GHOSTS

of Gettysburg

VI

Spirits, Apparitions and Haunted Places of the Battlefield

by

Mark V. Nesbitt

Second Chance Publications
Gettysburg, PA 17325

Published by   Second Chance Publications
P.O. Box 3126
Gettysburg, PA. 17325

ISBN 10: 0-9752836-0-X
ISBN 13: 978-0-9752836-0-8

Photos by the author unless otherwise credited.

To Frank Graziano

Teacher

Who once taught my class

*"It is not what exists that affects man
as much as what he <u>believes</u> to exist."*

.

We have done with Hope and Honor,
We are lost to Love and Truth,
We are dropping down the ladder rung by rung,
And the measure of our torment
Is the measure of our youth.
God help us, for we knew the worst too young!

–Rudyard Kipling

Table of Contents

Acknowledgments

Numerous people have helped in the gathering of these stories. Many have shared their fascinating, sometimes horrifying experiences with me, never expecting that they would be included in a book on the ghosts of Gettysburg. Others have lent support—mental, physical and emotional—in the arduous task it is to put together a book. To these people, my gratitude is given:

Linda Allewalt, Robin Bankert, Tessa Bardo, Joan and Dave Barr, Katie Bowman, Tom Bowman, Corinne Brownholtz, Rick Fisher, Michael J. Flood, John and Chris Gallagher, Michael Anne Hartmann, Ronnie Hull, Michael J. Isbansky, Fred and Robert Kerson, LaDonna King, Jeanne Knoop, Andrea Krcelic, Bill Lonecke, Renee and Leslie Ludwig, Melissa and Charles McGinnis, Colin and Karen Mehaffey, Dr. Dan Miller, Jennifer Moyer, Mistia Mullins, Jeneia Mullins, Ron and Barb Ogburn, Thomas W. Reidenbach, Sr., Jill Rider, Susan Robinson, Betty Jean Sanders, Ross and Nancy Simpson, Brandon K. Sloan, Michael Suarez, Jay Theisen, and Larry E. Werline.

Most importantly, I need to thank my wife of infinite patience, Carol, without whom all my writing would be just words on paper.

Introduction

Damned from Here to Eternity...

–Rudyard Kipling

The great William Shakespeare's play *Hamlet* is, in its essence, a ghost story. Young Prince Hamlet's boyhood is cut short not only by the murder of his father, the King, but also by the return of his father's ghost, beseeching him to avenge his murder. The King had been killed by his own brother for the throne. To make things worse, the murderer marries the queen—Hamlet's mother—within a month after the King's death.

Nearly all of Hamlet's actions in the play are driven by the literally haunting plea of his father's ghost to avenge his murder.

Some say the attempt to do the dead father's bidding drove the young Danish prince mad; it did result in his rejected betrothed's suicide, his killing of the Lord Chamberlain, and at the end of the play, in the deaths of Hamlet, his step-father/uncle, his mother, and his good friend. I may have missed one or two, for it is one of the bloodiest endings in all of Shakespeare.

But the key to the play comes in Act III, scene 3, when Hamlet stumbles upon his uncle—his father's killer—kneeling, his back turned, in prayer. Hamlet draws his sword and is about to dispatch his uncle into the Netherworld. Suddenly he stops. He sees a terrible irony:

Now might I do it pat, now he is praying.
And now I'll do it. And so he goes to heaven;
And so I am revenged. That would be scann'd;
A villain kills my father, and for that,
I, his sole son, do this same villain send to heaven.

Hamlet wants to kill him not while he is in prayer, assuring his spirit's passage into heaven, but rather when he is drunk or

7

gambling, swearing and raging, or during "some act that has no relish of salvation in it," so as to condemn him to Hell.

And it is in this decision that Hamlet also condemns himself. For in this one defining moment he goes from just wanting to kill his uncle, to judging him; from wanting merely to take his life to wanting to take his soul as well.

In one brief moment he goes from mortal man to aspiring to the power of God.

It is a moment upon which one of the greatest plays ever written turns; it may even be the moment upon which the great bard's play writing legacy turns. And for good reason: it is something we should all deeply ponder when we are thinking of the double-edged sword of revenge.

Even soldiers, whose job it is to kill, do not face that decision. To pull the trigger and take a human life, yes; to condemn a man's soul to eternal damnation, never.

And yet during the American Civil War, the men who fought, because of their religious convictions, no doubt wondered whether they were at times judges, or mere executioners.

There are a number of reasons, experts believe, why the human spirit remains bound to this earth after the death of the body. A sudden death is often mentioned. An unexpected, youthful extinction is another. A violent death, as well, will somehow leave the spirit behind at the site where its mortal vessel was shattered. The living, mourning too long for the dead is another reason for a haunting. Sometimes the spirit remains to give a message of hope, or a warning to those left behind.

One of the more ominous reasons accepted by experts as to why a human soul or spirit remains bound to earth is that person's fear of judgment.

This theory is backed up by the religious ritual of confession of and forgiveness for sins, especially at the time of death. If one is to face the Final Judge of all we've done in life, it is essential we go there penitent, as the poet Emily Dickinson wrote, "Beggars before the door of God."

So, if a youthful, sudden, unexpected, or violent death are also reasons souls remain rooted to earth, certainly the Battle of Gettysburg, during which nearly 100 percent of the deaths fit at least one of those categories, qualifies as a cause for any spirits being trapped here.

And if the men of Gettysburg were concerned about the fate of their own mortal souls as they were, in the heat of combat, setting the souls of their enemies free from their bodily prisons, then certainly it explains why so many have remained behind.

And if incessant mourning for the dead is a reason why spirits linger, with 1.6 million of us visiting Gettysburg yearly basically to remember and essentially mourn those who sacrificed here, still another condition for a haunting is satisfied.

And, as far as a message of hope, or warning? The warning is clear enough: do not make war, brother upon brother, for devastation is all you will reap.

And the message of hope may very well be that there is something of us that continues after death. As they are now, chained to the earth for who-knows-how-long, so, someday, may we be also.

Gettysburg Underground

...To where the damned have howled away their hearts,
And where the blessed dance....

–William Butler Yeats, "All Souls' Night"

There are worlds, access to which we are no longer allowed. Worlds just inches from us, as we stand in our own world. Invisible, they contain not only the present, but the past, and, some say, the future as well. Other generations of other ages apparently have been able to see into them: ancient shamans; some mystics in our age have; suffering saints, because of their strict aestheticism, have God's permission to go there; sometimes poets, who often suffer as much as saints, can peer into them as well. But we, convinced by those in our world that other worlds do not exist, have then convinced ourselves otherwise. And prison-pent we suffer the most exquisite torture of wondering....

For years—probably since before the great battle here—there have been nagging rumors of a strange subterranean complex—tunnels, if you will—below the streets of Gettysburg. I have spoken with visitors, long time residents, and local historians, and some too have heard the bizarre rumors. In the most famous small town in America, of which thousands of books have been written, no documentation for the underground grottoes can be found.

Yet one woman who grew up in Gettysburg from her birth, remembered a house mentioned in one of my previous *Ghosts of Gettysburg* books and recalled how, as children, she and a couple of her friends had somehow gotten into the basement of the house—perhaps shortly after the death of the elderly woman who had resided there—and found an entrance into what appeared to be a head-high (to a 10-year-old) secret shaft. Whether it had been boarded up and they removed the board on purpose, I do not know. I remember her saying that they began to enter and walk cautiously into the clammy darkness.

She said it headed off toward another house, not directly next door, but southward, under the back yard. It was either a dirt wall some several yards into the tunnel, or simply abject fear they ran into head-first that sent the children back to the cellar of the abandoned structure and up into the sunlight of a soft summer Gettysburg morning.

A local policeman—a high school classmate of the woman mentioned above—confirmed he too had heard of the tunnels and reminded me that the rumors have them starting below the Catholic Church on West High Street, coincidentally, during the battle, a field hospital. Interestingly, if one would draw a north-south line through the church it would bisect, generally, where my friend as a child explored to the limits of her fright, the mysterious tunnel in the basement.

Some have speculated that the tunnels were once part of the famous and clandestine Underground Railroad—therefore quite literally underground in Gettysburg—where runaway slaves would travel, scattering rodents before their feet, escaping from the dreaded "paterollers" and their dogs. Even in Gettysburg, seven miles north of the Mason-Dixon line, escaped slaves were not safe, thanks to the Fugitive Slave Act which made harboring an escapee illegal, even in "Free States."

If the catacombs were used for escaping slaves—or even if they merely exist—they might very well be a treasure-trove for archaeologists and historians.

Some also have said that the subterranean tunnels sheltered soldiers: Union soldiers escaping from Confederates after being driven from their positions on the first day of fighting; Confederates who had been wounded or were merely curious as to what lay hidden underneath their feet; surgeons and orderlies, dressed in their white dusters preparing to operate upon the wounded in the clandestine hospital.

One such orderly who served in Gettysburg would go on to a more notorious infamy.

Lewis Thornton Powell (aka Lewis Paine) fought at Gettysburg in a Florida Regiment. At 6' 1" and 175 pounds he made a big target and was wounded in the battle and captured. Only slightly hurt, he was put to work in "Old Dorm," now known as Pennsylvania Hall, on the Gettysburg College Campus. His stint as a white-coated orderly was short-lived. As soon as he could, he escaped from his Yankee captors. Having access to the cellar of the old building, did he also find access to the underground warrens to explore and plant the seed of escape from his captors? (For that matter, could some subterranean conduit be the means by which the wraiths of long-dead surgeons, orderlies and wounded appear and vanish seemingly at will in the cellar of Old Dorm?)[1]

He was sent to Baltimore and did escape and his escape helped mold a strange twist in American History. Somehow at the end of the war he got tangled up with a young and famous actor, soon to be infamous. With his association with one John Wilkes Booth, Powell/Paine would become a co-conspirator in the assassination of Abraham Lincoln by viciously stabbing Secretary of State William Seward numerous times the same night of the assassination. One source has him shouting as he ran from the bloody scene he had created, "Mad! I am mad!" Powell would hang for his role, but numerous photos would be taken of him while he was in prison dressed up in what appears to be a long, light-colored coat and hat for identification by witnesses. Was he ever a denizen of the alleged underground passages beneath Gettysburg? An even more tantalizing question emerges: If he did use the subterranean burrows at one time, could he have returned...even after his hanging in 1865?

Wild, unsubstantiated, recent rumors have the tunnels as a conduit for illegal activities of unknown nature in small-town Gettysburg: let the reader's imagination fill in the details....

Still others maintain that the grottoes would provide excellent passages for perturbed, restless, unsettled spirits, remaining from Gettysburg's earliest times, through which they could move from haunted site to haunted site. This would be especially true if they were built—inadvertently or on purpose—along "ley lines," those energy paths that occur naturally in the earth.

One can only imagine the spirits of Gettysburg's ancient dead descending from their graves above to the underground tunnels, then floating silently, wispily, along passageways through the underworld, to emerge as from some supernatural subway, passing through rock and concrete and wood as they are wont to do, and materializing at times of their own choosing, at those most famous haunted places such as the Codori or Culp Houses, Devil's Den, or the Triangular Field, or Spangler's Spring, where they may bubble up from the earth like the water that seems to help draw them. Then, as they appeared, so they disappear, sinking back into their labyrinthine warrens, to move, undetected, just inches below the living. And this they do at their own whim, or perhaps when some living human in need beckons them in just the right way....

There is a house on a melancholy street in Gettysburg, close enough to the college (and also Old Dorm) so as to have been used for nearly thirty years as student housing. It has been the scene of serious studies by aspiring intellectuals, of raucous parties filled to the brim with youthful enthusiasm. It has been the living quarters of scores of lively students, of scholars and athletes vital with the ebullience and perceived invulnerability of youth. It has also been the dwelling place of Death.

At first it was the site. The roads coming in from the east and west actually struck the main road within a few blocks, and when the Union line imploded on the afternoon of July 1, 1863, sons of the North ran helter-skelter for their very lives through the space now occupied by the house. A battery of Union artillery established a temporary line straddling the road and hot shell and sighing canister blew through the space the house would some day occupy. Southern men were sliced open by the blunt canister balls traveling faster than the speed of sound. Yankees were shot through the lungs and spine and kidneys from behind as their rebel counterparts chased them down the dirt road past where the house now stands. Death has been no stranger to the site upon which the house sits or even it's subsurface (if those reports of underground tunnels in that area of Gettysburg are true).

Nor has Death, who washes away this worrisome world, been estranged to the brick walls and wooden trim that circumscribe the space where men once reluctantly traded their mortal existence for existence on another plane.

And while students for the last several years have pursued their goals—intellectual and social—within the walls of the house, there was a persistent rumor of a malevolent visitor to the house who was not a student at all, who had an agenda of pursuit and manipulation for evil all his own.

According to the few descriptions left of him, he was young—in his late twenties—and dressed in white—perhaps a lab coat from a college science classroom, or something out of a century-old photo of doctors or orderlies or embalmers—and he was, or appeared to be, quite mad.

Angry at something, yes. But mad also in the Victorian sense of the word: mentally deranged. He would appear in the house, wander aimlessly, move to the door to the basement, and when curious students would go to find him, be gone.

He was apparently darkly handsome as well, with deep-set, mysterious eyes, a squared off jaw and thick dark hair. A matinee idol…but of a different age.

There is a theory in parapsychology that explains strange behavior in certain people: madness, suicidal tendencies, bizarre irritability, unexplainable outbursts or uncharacteristic behavior. It is similar to a possession, except that, instead of the devil taking over someone's body, it is the spirit of a dead individual that enters and takes over. It is called a "walk-in." The most frightening aspect of it is that sometimes you can tell when a person is the victim of a walk-in because of their radical change—but sometimes you cannot.

It cannot be assumed that the individual actually lived in the house. Or, better put, it cannot be assumed that the individual "lived" while he was in the house. It also cannot be assumed that he is completely gone from the house either. Some stories have him killing himself in that basement. Others say he was already dead—an apparition in a long, white coat—when he hanged himself, using the act as an enticement for others to follow and as a demonstration for how easy it is to self-immolate. Or perhaps he was seen reenacting his own fate on a government gallows a dozen decades past....

They say a note was left explaining unexplainable actions. Yet officials have not—nor, I surmise, ever will—reveal its contents. I have heard rumors though. Perhaps in the note there is reference to the former tenant who wailed his own life away within the ever-narrowing confines of the walls; or a reference to joining the infamous "man-in-white" who apparently still lives—if that is the right word for it—in the cellar. The history of the house revealed that, indeed, a second person succumbed to the same manner of endless sleep, accomplishing "the thing that ends all other deeds."

One who spoke under strict oath of anonymity questioned whether anyone should even be allowed to live in the house "if there's that kind of spirit still involved in the house. If there is such a thing as being 'called'—if you are in a vulnerable space—by a negative spirit, well...."

Two self-appointed encounters with the Great Imposter within the same confines of the same walls on that lonely corner in Gettysburg can only be a convergence beyond coincidence, beyond understanding, and perhaps, beyond this world.

Unquiet Rest

After conducting just ten people through the process of visionary facilitation, I realized it was possible to duplicate the common human experience of seeing apparitions of the deceased. Of the ten I ushered through the process, five saw apparitions of their departed relatives. Later, after improving my facilities and refining my technique, I conducted visionary facilitations with even better results.

–Raymond Moody, M.D. *Reunions*

During the Civil War it was relatively rare for fighting to occur at night. With communications as they were in the 19th Century, it was almost impossible to know what your own troops—let alone the enemy—were doing. Yet, even without fighting, nightfall on the field of combat was a time fraught with horrors.

Of course there were the noises: myriad and terror-filled cries of the wounded and dying echoing long and pitifully into the night; the disembodied rumblings from the enemy lines of men and artillery being moved from place to an even more threatening place; and what may be the worst, that little mysterious, unidentifiable rustling in the darkness just behind your shoulder that could be an enemy soldier ready to run you through with a bayonet…or a mere chipmunk.

Actually fighting in the dark through the claustrophobic woodlands and rock-ridden farm fields that were the battlefields of America in the mid-19th Century was unthinkably horrible. Yet at Gettysburg the most horrible occurred.

Because of the late start of the assaults, the fighting around Culp's Hill and East Cemetery Hill dragged on into the darkness of July 2, 1863. On the hill named after the farm family who owned much of it, the fighting died down after dark, to result in blind firing through most of the night. It flared up again into full-scale combat near daylight. In the darkened woods of Culp's Hill, for a few desperate hours in American History, it was the soldiers' special Hell.[1]

Men fired at musket flashes and sounds ahead of them, never really knowing if they were killing friend or foe. You never knew, in the smoke that hung beneath the trees in the dark, when you were going to walk right into the muzzle of an enemy musket. The threat was real: for a while Confederates actually took over abandoned Union breastworks and when the Union troops returned there was the dark melee, horrifying screams in the night, and men dying suddenly and violently.

Night is always a time of icy fear and apprehension. It must stem from our most primal subconscious, harkening back to when we were cave-dwellers, scurrying about for millennia, when our only occupation was to avoid being prey. At night our sense of sight—perhaps our most keen sense—is in it's most disadvantaged environment. Day brings knowledge; in a hostile setting, it brings life. Night can bring sudden death—as it did during the inky black of a sultry summer's night on Cemetery and Culp's Hills—or it can bring much worse. And sleep, if it should come, steals consciousness, our last warning system, and makes us more vulnerable to earthly creatures that would do us harm.

Or to other entities not of this earth with perhaps the same ambition.

The ancient Greeks believed that sleep was the main portal through which ghosts came into their lives.[2] In the hundreds of stories I have documented about living humans' encounters with dead ones, scores have happened at night.

It is well known that possessions, walk-ins, apparitions, and other psychic intrusions often come when we are supposed to be safe and sound—in our sleep.

Some studies have indicated that during certain realms of sleep we dream, and in dreaming allow a conduit for thoughts and ideas which come not from the safety of our own subconscious, but from others' minds as well—others both living and dead. *Something awakens you from a fitful sleep. You roll over in your bed and there, right at the foot of it, is a misty shape resembling a human. But its features are hazy, unclear. The dress it wears is recognizable, but from an era long past, and it is tattered, as if it had spent too much time hanging in a closet, or lying in the damp mustiness of a coffin. The figure is, at first, an object of curiosity, since you immediately assume you're dreaming. But its tendril-like arms begin to wave, to move towards you—no, to beckon you—and the face twists into the mockery of a smile. Now you begin to panic as you realize—despite your hoping it's not true—that you are fully awake, that this is no dream and there is no explanation for the horrid sight before you, except that it is real, in all its dead splendor....*

Because Gettysburg's main industry since the battle has been tourism, the town and its environs have sprouted hotels, motels and bed & breakfasts to accommodate those who wish to stay overnight. As a matter of fact, you may be reading these words from the comfort of one of Gettysburg's fine rooms at this very moment....

The motels and hotels where our visitors sleep are always clean—competition is tough so they all must rise to the occasion. Yet nearly all are built on pieces of land that once felt the trod of panicked, desperate men, or upon earth that caressed the faces of the fallen. There, in the very space where you sleep (or lie down to read this book), passed an ancient soldier, either fleeing Death or caught in his icy grasp. Where you lay your body to rest for the night, some soldier lay down to rest until the end of life.

Perhaps that is why so many who have stayed in the local inns have experienced eerie reminders of those who once lived, struggled and perished here....

A man who has been a reenactor and visits Gettysburg frequently wrote to tell of several unexplainable happenings, beginning first with his attendance at a reenactment in the early 1990s. He told of himself as well as others in the camp at night hearing the out-of-time sounds of numerous soldiers marching through some distant woods. One night, from across the fields where battlelines once advanced, rolled a fog unlike he'd ever seen before; and from within that creeping fog came sounds: the hoof beats of horses, hundreds of shuffling feet, and equipment clanking together as it had when living men marched through the same woods and fields.

Other times he recalled smelling pipe smoke on an abandoned Baltimore Street near where Mary Virginia Wade, the only civilian killed by the maelstrom outside her door, took her last startled breath. And he felt the cold spots out in front of Virginia's monument to her fallen sons at Gettysburg, in the fields across which Pickett's doomed men sought victory and glory…and found death and glory.

But the title "Pickett's Charge," is a great misnomer. What has come down to us as "Pickett's Charge," the military assault that became a symbol of shattered hopes and mass slaughter, was actually made up not only of Pickett's Division, but brigades from three other Divisions—Anderson, Heth (commanded by Pettigrew) and Pender's. In fact, with apologies to Virginians who would garner all the dubious, bloody glory for Pickett's Charge, there were at least fifteen North Carolina regiments that participated in the charge. The two brigades of Pender's Division, which were engaged, were Scales and Lane's brigades, composed exclusively of ten North Carolina regiments. And the "Tarheels" will not be forgotten— evidently, not even to this day.

Our reenactor/correspondent and his family always stayed at the Home Sweet Home Motel, just on the edge of the fields where Pender and Pettigrew's men advanced. In fact, Lane's

Brigade of North Carolinians appears to have passed closest to where our correspondent and his family slept—fitfully, as it turned out.

The first night there, he and his wife were awakened by a soft jingling sound like someone playing with the change they had left on the dresser.[3] Turning on a light and expecting to see a mouse...they saw nothing. The very moment the light went out, the sound started again, but from a different area of the room. Around and around the room the unexplainable jingling went, pausing first in one corner, then at another wall, until the sound was right next to the bed. Then it became a plopping sound like water dripping. Indeed his wife had left a cup of coffee—the Civil War soldiers' favorite beverage—next to the bed. After thirty minutes, the sound ended...only to begin again the next night. Three out of the four nights they stayed in that room, the nocturnal visitors tarried for their allotted time, only to leave abruptly when that time was up.

Site of Home Sweet Home and Long Lane.

The family returned seven months later and, in spite of perhaps having to share accommodations with an unseen boarder, they requested the same room they'd had before. Again, late at night, came evidence of their visitor. Our correspondent had left a Rand McNally Atlas on a chair. At 4:00 A.M. he was awakened by the sound of paper shuffling, like the sound of the pages of a book being turned and examined. The noise was brief and he fell back to sleep.

He awoke again at 6:00 A.M. for the day. The Atlas, instead of lying on the chair where he had left it the night before, was on the floor at the foot of the bed.

The pages were open to North Carolina.

Sadly, however, it will be the last time the peripatetic spirit of some North Carolina soldier will pass through an odd-looking (to him) overnight accommodation, and the last time he will be able to look longingly there at a map of his home in the Old North State. If he is granted another visit to this earth, he will be disappointed in the accommodations...or will perhaps, recognize to his horror, the very earth upon which he bled and died. You see, the National Park Service purchased the Home Sweet Home and tore it down in the spring of 2003.

Dr. Raymond Moody, author of several books on communicating with the dead, re-discovered an ancient technique enabling one to see visions of the dead. Basing his work on research into the past, of shamans, Celts and Medieval England, he created what he called a "psychomanteum"—a room in which, under certain conditions, while gazing into a mirror, apparitions of dead relatives can be seen. The ancients used other similar reflective instruments—cauldrons filled with oil or water, silver cups filled with blood, polished obsidian—to "divine" the future.[4]

Yet who would ever think that one of the finely appointed, modern motel rooms in Gettysburg would, upon a certain occasion, become a chamber wherein the dead could be seen again?

Two brothers had stayed in one particular motel several times over the years. And while some motels claim to be next to the battlefield, most are really "on" the battlefield since the soldiers did not look into the future and see the boundaries of the National Park that was to be here one day, stop and say, "We cannot fight beyond this line, for this is where a great battlefield Park will be established someday and we must fight our battle within those boundaries and no further."[5] Obviously, the fighting took them wherever Fate will.

One night in the room they placed a chair against the door as an added safety measure from intruders. Late into the night one of the brothers was awakened by the loud rattling of the door and the chair. His brother heard the same sound. He checked the front porch from the window but no one was there. Anyone trying to enter by mistake would not have rattled the door since that motel uses plastic cards for keys. But an outside intruder was disqualified immediately: frighteningly, the sound came from inside the room and not outside the door. It was as if someone was trying to get out of the room, not in.

The next morning he inspected the chair and found that somehow it had been pulled out, away from the door about an inch.

His brother then related to him something that had happened to him when he awoke in the middle of the night. The room was dimly illuminated by a faint, green-glowing nightlight. On the wall hangs a mirror, into which the light casts its luminescence. In a semi-awakened state he gazed into the mirror and saw the reflected light begin to take the shape of a woman dressed in a print dress from the mid-19th Century era. As he continued to stare at the apparition in the mirror, she was suddenly accompanied by a man dressed as a cavalryman, complete with high cavalry boots.

After his experience in the makeshift psychomanteum, sleep was laborious. While tossing and turning he began hearing certain seemingly impossible sounds: outside in the distance, the boom of cannon; a bugle mournfully playing; the metallic clash of crossed sabers. Impossible sounds indeed...except at Gettysburg.

And finally the spirits drew blood.

As they were packing up and leaving Gettysburg, his brother took a disposable razor by the handle and tossed it into the wastebasket. The moment it hit the basket, a small cut appeared on his other hand. It bled and ached for a good part of their ride home.

At another motel in the same vicinity, in January 1998, a young man and his family were spending the night during what is usually a very quiet time of year in Gettysburg. Sometime between two and four in the morning the young man was awakened by the sound of artillery firing from the area known as the High Water Mark. He described the sound as cannons firing "by piece," or one-at-a-time. He apparently could hear them re-loading between shots. The fire lasted about ten minutes, then faded out, back into some mysterious fold of Time. Frightened, he did not look outside. He woke his parents in the middle of the night to ask if they had heard it. Unfortunately, they had been sound asleep and did not. In a post-script he mentioned that he did not believe the sounds were a figment of his imagination.

A woman was staying with her husband in one of the finest bed & breakfasts in the area. It seems a bit out of town, but is situated on one of the roads along which many of the field hospitals were located shortly after the battle. But that bed & breakfast serves as the venue for a most remarkable connection between the dead and the living which seems to have spanned the ages.

The woman is an historian working in Charleston, South Carolina. Charleston, depending with whom you speak, was either the hotbed of rebellion, or the birthplace of the struggle for Southern rights and independence. Regardless, it is a magnificent, history-filled city, reborn, literally, from the ashes of its past and the longest, continuous, daily artillery bombardment—545 straight days—ever suffered on the North American Continent.[6]

The woman was visiting Gettysburg during the winter, this time for a very specific, personal reason: she wished to follow in the final footsteps of an ancestor who fought with the 15th South Carolina in Kershaw's Brigade and was killed in action at Gettysburg. She and her husband had settled in for the evening and were lying in bed. She tried to sleep, but there was an odd noise that echoed across the fields between the bed & breakfast and the battlefield. Faint at first, the sound was soon recognizable: from another era: drumbeats.

She finally fell asleep, never understanding the source of the sound that once rallied men for battle a century-and-a-third before. But even in sleep she found no comfort.

It was the most vivid dream she's ever had, so real she wrote she could still feel it two years afterwards. In her dream she was running forward. There was an icy apprehension as she ran forward, she stated, as if she were running for her life. She came to a small stream and crossed it. She felt the sharp coldness of the water, but she somehow knew she had to get across. "The fear was terrible," she wrote.

The next day she and her husband drove the approximate route Kershaw's men traveled—including her own cousin—as they marched inexorably to their doom. As they came around a curve, suddenly she realized she was staring at the water she had crossed the night before in her dream. It was a branch of Plum Run, also known as "Bloody Run," re-named because, for a few horrifying hours in southern history, it literally ran red, its waters tainted by South Carolinians—and multitudes of others—who re-christened it with their life's blood.

"I am a working historian in a museum house here in Charleston," she wrote, "and my business is fact, not imagination, but I believe cousin John sent that dream that winter night." She comes from a very old southern family, rich with stories of their past. Gettysburg, for some reason, fascinated her more than any other battle of the "War for Southern Independence."

"I believe," she continued, "that the passionate interest I have in the battle somehow weakened the barrier between my cousin and me, allowing us somehow to touch each other in a most unusual way."

It is not such a great barrier, this thin, misty line between life and death. It has been breached at certain times and in certain places. No doubt there is a long link between generations, passed down unmistakably by the very DNA we hold within our cells. Is this connection enough to help "cross over?" So many of those encounters have been documented that entire books have been written about the ease with which we can see or hear or feel those who have passed before us. Why, we ourselves can go there anytime we wish and as quickly as we wish. There's only one hitch: the return trip is most difficult.

Another motel on the edge of the National Park has a series of beautiful suites available to the visitors. At the beginning of May 1999, a man and his girlfriend were enjoying the experience of visiting Gettysburg. But for one night in their suite, their Gettysburg experience took a weird turn.

It was midnight. As they were preparing to retire for the night, the electrical power in their suite was suddenly reduced to a "brown-out." The television and digital clocks stopped working and the lights produced a mere flicker. They called the front desk and the clerk came over to check the fuse-box in the basement. That, he assured them, was not the source of the power "brown-out," and also informed them that theirs was the only suite to lose power. Indeed, they could see lights in the surrounding buildings, including the one right next door. The clerk explained that there was nothing that could be done until the maintenance crew came the next morning and graciously gave them a key to a nearby suite that had power in case they wanted to move. They decided to remain where they were, opening the shades to let a little of the street lighting into the room.

Around two in the morning both were awakened by a loud thump from the attic above their heads. It sounded as if something weighing several pounds hit the attic floor. They waited anxiously for another indication of a prowler, or animal, or anything logical to explain the noise. Not another sound was heard, and so they nervously drifted back off to uneasy sleep.

At 3:00 A.M. the man was in the bathroom when the power came back on. The lights brightened to full intensity in the bathroom and he could distinctly hear what sounded like the television coming back on: there were muffled voices in conversation coming from the bedroom. He reasoned that the TV would awaken his girlfriend and she would turn it off. But as he began closing the blinds in the bathroom, which they had opened earlier in the evening, he realized that she hadn't arisen.

He entered the bedroom and saw that she was still sound asleep and had not moved. He went to turn off the TV but was surprised that it was not on. Grateful to have the power back on and not giving the sounds he had heard earlier a second thought, he went back to bed and was soon asleep.

The next morning they peeked into the attic to see what had fallen and were shocked to see that there was nothing on the floor of the attic that could have produced the sound. As he told her about the sounds he had heard emanating from the bedroom in the middle of the night, they both suddenly realized that the TV had never been on, and, since there were no occupants of the suite next door to theirs, the strange murmuring sounds he had heard so clearly the night before could have no explainable source.

Inquiring at the front desk of the motel as to the power brown-out, they received three answers: first, that the entire area may have been afflicted with the brown-out, which they knew was not the case since surrounding buildings were unaffected; second, that there may have been a car accident that took out a pole and caused the power to fail—but that again would have affected all the lights in the area, and clearly the street lights had been on all night. The third explanation, as illogical as it may seem, provided perhaps the most logical—perhaps the only—explanation for the strange power outage and the bizarre conversation he heard in the bedroom. They were told that it was most likely the work of the ghosts who also spend their days and nights in the building.

As well, the couple admitted a revelation on the trip home. Unbeknownst to both, each had separately experienced a series of "uneasy feelings" in the closet beneath the kitchen stairs.

(While writing this story, as I was preparing to put the letter back in its envelope, I realized there were a handwritten note and a photo that I had overlooked before. The note explained that just as they were about to mail the letter they had their film of the trip developed. There is a shot of the window in the bath and to the right of it a strange, formed haze. I have seen these before, especially where there is a mirror in the room and visible in the picture, as in bathrooms and bedrooms. The "ghost" is merely the flash hitting the mirror and reflecting eerily on the wall. But this photo is different. There is no mirror or reflective surface to produce the haze. A description in the note states that they see in the haze the visage of a young man with brown hair and a moustache, sideburn in front of his left ear, with his eyes gazing to the right.)

In a different part of the same motel and at another time a man and his wife were spending the night. He is an avid Civil War buff, and an officer of his local Civil War Round Table. They had turned in for the night and apparently had gotten some sleep, when he said he dreamed (and, in his letter, placed three question marks behind the word 'dreamed' as if he was not sure if he had dreamed it or it was real) that he saw a woman walk through the room and into the bathroom. He described her as about 5'3" and moving at a fast walk past the foot of their bed. She had light-colored hair and seemed in a hurry to finish dressing since she wore just a short skirt that came to above the knees and a bra. The short skirt and hairstyle reminded the man of the 1960s or 70s. He said he dreamed (once again with several question marks) that he sat up as she walked by and when she had passed, he lay down again to fall back asleep.

He woke about 6:30 the next morning and, while his wife slept, shaved and showered. While shaving he had the strange feeling that he was not alone. His attention was drawn to his wife's opal ring that lay on a glass shelf above the sink. He stepped out of the bathroom to retrieve something, turned immediately back into the bathroom and noticed at once that the ring was gone. He was dumbfounded: he hadn't touched the glass shelf and so it was impossible that he had knocked it off. He looked around the sink, then to either side of the sink on the floor, but couldn't find the ring.

When any of us search for something missing, we check all the logical places first. After those are examined, then we begin to search some of the more illogical, impossible places. So it was with this gentleman. After all logical places had been searched; he finally reached directly under the sink and pulled out the empty wastebasket. There, in the bottom, was the ring.

He stated that even if he had knocked the ring off the shelf, it would have to have broken all the laws of physics for it to fall *around* the sink, curve in its fall to end up *under* the sink and land in the wastebasket. It was as if it had somehow passed through the sink and into the basket. The only other possible explanation was that someone had taken it from the shelf and placed it in the wastebasket…someone, of course, who was completely invisible.

As soon as he found the ring, the uncomfortable feeling of not being alone disappeared.

In the annals of the supernatural, there are countless tales of 'apports' or the sudden appearance of physical items 'out of thin air' or passing through solid objects into the viewer's realm. In my experience there is the psychic whose dead relative passed her a handkerchief with his image upon it; the soldier on Little Round Top who passed two cartridges to a reenactor; and the following:

I received another letter from a man who claimed that while his wife is a firm believer in the supernatural, he has never been. But something happened to completely change his way of thinking recently; and it happened on the battlefield of Gettysburg.

On a visit to the famous and once deadly Wheatfield, his wife collected some seedlings from the majestic cedar trees that grow wild in the field. Returning to the motel she wrapped the seedlings in a damp paper towel to preserve them for the ride home. Later that evening after dark, they returned to the Wheatfield, admittedly, to see if they could experience something of the supernatural.

A car pulled up behind them and a couple got out. They were obviously 'ghost hunting' since they carried a thermal scanner, and began to take numerous photos around a large cedar tree. While watching the couple, the man thought he saw something out of his peripheral vision move to his left. He concentrated on the area, but in the darkened fields of battle, once crawling with wounded men and boys, failed to see any other movement. The two investigators returned from the cedar tree in the Wheatfield and the two couples began to chat. It was November and the air in the Wheatfield seemed a little more damp and chilly than the surrounding area. The man put his hand in his wife's jean pocket for warmth, but when he pulled it out, a small, gold nugget, pinky ring slipped from his finger. He told her that his ring had just ended up in her pocket, but search as she might, the ring wasn't there. No one had heard it hit the pavement, yet they searched with flashlights in vain for several more minutes. Frustrated, they left the battlefield.

When the couple got back to their motel room, the wife searched again in her jean cuff, pockets, and clothing for the ring, in case it had gotten caught. That search too, was in vain.

Preparing for bed, they decided they would travel to the Wheatfield one more time in the morning to search for the ring before they left. The wife also expressed an interest in retrieving 2 or 3 more cedar seedlings.

It was the middle of the night. The husband was awakened by his wife talking in her sleep. Clearly she was communicating with someone unseen, who had entered, unbidden into her mind, to proffer some otherworldly bargain. "If you bring it back," her husband heard her say distinctly, "I promise I won't get any more trees."

The next morning they awoke, showered, dressed and packed the car. Before returning the room key he asked his wife to check the room to make sure they'd gotten everything. She said she thought they'd gotten everything, but to assure him she went back in.

From the room he heard his wife exclaim, "Honey, look!" As he walked into the room she was picking up the lost nugget ring from a spot obvious enough to have been seen as they were packing.

The man admitted in the letter that after his wife's 'deal' made in her sleep and its results, his belief in the supernatural has increased considerably.

*   *   *

I was about twelve years old, so it comes to me now almost like a dream. My family was visiting the town of Sharpsburg, Maryland, the surrounding fields of which became some of the most blood-soaked land on earth during the daylight hours of September 17, 1862. Called the Battle of Antietam in the north and Sharpsburg in the south, it was the bloodiest single day in all of American history. We had entered a small, privately owned museum in town. Though I was the last to enter the room, I was the first to see it. There, hanging on the wall, was a shriveled, mummified, human arm. The skin, like parchment, wrapped itself in wrinkling folds around the articulated bones and what was left of the desiccated muscles. The hand was withered to the bone and bent back in an unnatural angle, a contorted claw. It brought to me then, and continues to present to this day, nightmarish reminders of the power of Civil War artillery, to blow off a limb like that, or the hideous precision of a mid-19th Century surgeon, to amputate some boy's cherished limb.

I received a 12-page letter from an historian, whom I had met at one of my signings at the *Ghosts of Gettysburg Candlelight Walking Tours*® Headquarters. He wrote that he found my books "relieving" because he had been experiencing some unexplainable events himself and thought that his imagination might have been acting up. His next statement could very well be one of the truest ever written: "Many things have a logical explanation but there are many things that do not."

He went on to say that because of his religious training, he has long realized that there is another life besides just the corporeal one we all share and that his religion accepts an afterlife and the existence of a spiritual soul. In fact, he could be writing from nearly any religious point of view since virtually every major religion on the face of the earth believes in some sort of afterlife.

In his research as an historian, he has interviewed numerous curators of historical sites and they have confided in him that indeed the unexplainable—perhaps even the paranormal—has occurred at the places where they work. He has come to realize that the scene of a great tragedy often becomes the scene of great hauntings, although he himself had never experienced anything out of the ordinary in his many previous visits to Gettysburg. He thought that it was because he always felt deep sympathy for those who made the sacrifice at Gettysburg and would often recite the traditional prayers for the dead while visiting sites of great carnage. One night in Gettysburg, however, his lack of experience with the paranormal would come to an abrupt halt.

He came to Gettysburg with his brother and stayed in one of the motels. After an enjoyable day of touring, they retired for the evening. Habitually he carries with him a couple of small prayer books that he binds together with a rubber band. They were in place on the nightstand next to his bed. All was quiet, yet, unbeknownst to him, his sleep was about to be interrupted by an intrusion from another world.

At about three in the morning, while lying on his side, he was awakened by a rough shove on his shoulder, so forceful that it pushed him onto his stomach. He turned to see what his brother wanted. Instead of his sibling, he was astonished to see, floating before his eyes, a white, glowing, disembodied arm pull back and vanish into the darkness of the room. Startled, he sat up and looked around. His brother was still sound asleep in the other bed. Everything was quiet in the room and outside. Nothing was out of place. At first he thought it might have been a dream, but the shove was real…and so was the sight of the arm receding back into whatever world from whence it came. After several futile attempts at slumber, somehow he managed to fall back to sleep.

Then, about an hour later, he was awakened by a bizarre sound in the room. As he listened in the dark, he identified the sound as a 'popping,' or 'snapping.' By now he was wide-awake and began to try to listen more closely and locate the source. In a moment, there was another 'pop.' A few more seconds passed. Another 'snap.' Another second or two passed. Another 'pop.'

In all there were five or six of the odd sounds before he finally realized where they were coming from: right behind his head on the nightstand. Within mere inches of his face, someone was playing with the rubber bands holding his prayer books together.

He was certain that his brother was not playing with the books at that hour, but he began to sit up and roll over anyway to be certain. As he did, he felt a strong hand grab him by the shoulder and shake him violently as if to wake him. He turned suddenly and there it was again: the deathly white, bodiless arm, retreating back into the abyss of darkness in the room.

He described the bloodless limb as "glowing a soft fluorescent white. The hand and forearm looked delicate and slender. I think it was that of a young woman. If it was a man's arm I would have to guess that it was that of a younger fellow."

As the arm pulled away he clearly saw that it ended at the elbow, as if it had been surgically amputated. By this time the man was as annoyed as he was frightened, and shouted at the hideous thing to get out of the room and leave him alone. He looked at his brother, but even his outburst failed to awaken him.

It was the last time the amputated limb would appear that night.

The next morning, before he could say anything, his brother awoke in an agitated mood and asked him why he kept trying to awaken him. Incredulously, his brother proceeded to tell him that on two occasions he was shaken awake by the shoulder, but was too tired to respond. Instead he just mumbled to "stop playing games," and fell back to sleep without investigating.

The correspondent summed it up like this:

"What happened to me that night? Someone suggested that it was common for soldiers to wake up their buddies when it was time to go out on picket duty.... As to the rubber band snapping I heard that ghosts are sometimes amused and puzzled by things they find that were not common to their time and sometimes play around with them out of curiosity."

Now disembodied arms disappearing into the darkness of a strange motel room may seem a bit much, perhaps even unbelievable. I thought so too, except for his obvious skepticism, sincerity, and his attempt to put it all into perspective using his knowledge and reasoning powers.

And because of another e-mail I received while writing this chapter.

A woman and her husband were staying at one of the town's finer bed & breakfasts. She has been a frequent visitor to Gettysburg, coming to visit the town and battlefield about five times a year for the last eight years. She's stayed at many of the local bed & breakfasts and hotels. Nothing out of the ordinary had happened to her in all those visits. Until the latest.

They had retired for the evening. They had never stayed in this particular room in the bed & breakfast. She was dozing off to sleep when she felt what she thought was her cat from home lying down on the end of the bed. Then it dawned on her: she wasn't at home, but in Gettysburg. She looked to the foot of the bed and there was nothing. She mentally shrugged it off and went back to sleep.

Within a short while she was awakened again, this time by the covers being pulled over her head. Pushing them back down, she looked over at her husband, but he was sound asleep, snoring. She admits to having been a little "spooked," and lying awake for a long while. Just as she began to feel comfortable, it happened again: the covers whipped over her head. Again, after several minutes, she calmed herself and managed to fall back asleep.

At 4:00 A.M. she was awakened by her husband moving in his sleep. He was rubbing his face against his pillow as if he were trying to remove something stubborn clinging to it. Still asleep, he lifted his hand as if to shoo something away from his face. It was then she saw it.

Extending across her body just inches from her face and draped with what looked like some lacy fabric, was a woman's arm, from the elbow down, the pale fingers eerily entwined in her husband's hair, tousling it playfully. She screamed, awakening her husband, and the phantom limb disappeared. She shouted to him that they were not alone in that room. In the partial stupor of sleep, he hadn't comprehended what she had meant, looked around and saw no one, and told her to go back to sleep.

Fitful sleep followed until about 7:00 A.M. when she was again awakened by someone blowing gently on her face. She realized that she was facing away from her husband, so it couldn't have been him. Frustrated with trying to sleep in that room, she arose and showered.

Upon awakening, her husband was strangely silent, and continued to be after he showered and began to dress. Suddenly he asked her about the small, blue pillow that was on the bed and if she had moved it? She answered no. He said that when he had gotten up it was in the center of the bed. Now, it was clearly at the head of the bed, next to the headboard. They both stood in silence for a moment until he finally said, "Get your stuff packed and let's get out of here!"

He refused to talk about it until they got into the car. On the way home she told him all that had happened through the night and asked him if he believed her. He said he wouldn't have if it wasn't for the pillow incident, and if he hadn't felt something strange after she screamed in the middle of the night. She asked him what that was. He said that after she screamed he had felt something push down on the bed as if someone was getting into it.

In a follow-up e-mail, her impression of the incident was a speculation that the entity was a female, perhaps taking care of someone who was sick. That is why they kept feeling someone sitting on the bed. Her explanation of why the covers continued to be pulled over her head is a little more ominous: she felt the person being cared for had died, thus explaining the shrouding of the face. She talked to her husband again to see if he remembered any more and he said he could add only one more thing.

His overwhelming feeling was simply "to get the hell out of there."

Phantom limbs hovering over us, or playfully touching, or roughly shoving us. What could it be that allows the many manifestations of an active, viable, yet impossible world, sometimes seen, more often unseen, that apparently exists right next to us? What aberration in Time or Physics or Mass or Energy reveals to us this other land, usually unheard and invisible, that seems the dwelling-place of the dead?

.

Time's Pawns

Historians love to play the game, "What if they invented a Time Machine?"

Some of us who are old enough to remember the *Rocky & Bullwinkle Show* might recall Mr. Peabody, the talking, bespectacled dog with an I.Q. of Einstein. He had a "pet" boy named Sherman, and, to explore some mystery of the past for the benefit of the children watching, they would climb into a device Mr. Peabody had invented called the "Wayback Machine," which would transport them to any historical time period they desired.

That was kid's stuff, right? Yet science and some pretty influential physicists have pondered hard on the possibilities—and ramifications—of returning to the past. Some shrug it off as impossible, since time is a continuum and there is no going back...or forward, for that matter. Some say that all time is contained in the past and there is literally no future. Others bode ominously that even our merest presence in the past would disrupt the continuum and set up an entirely new future—where we live now—and change things so that the present is not what it is, perhaps even leading to the possibility that the time traveler into the past might never have even been born!

Still others claim time travel has already been accomplished and proven by sound physical laws.

The Nazis, according to at least one writer, had a super-secret facility located in a mine in Poland in which they conducted experiments using rare metals spinning at tremendous speeds in opposite directions. The result was the creation of a "field"—a "torsion field"—within whose influence strange things occurred. One thing was the rapid disintegration of life forms within the field's influence. The Nazis had experimented with plants, mice, and, considering the Nazis, probably humans. The other result, if the torsion field is strong enough, is the disruption or bending of space. And, because of the space-time continuum—a well-known and accepted inviolable connection between space and time—if space is bent or distorted, so is time. A slowing or stoppage of time is the result.[1]

Not exactly a "Wayback Machine," but the description of a torsion field leads to an unusual connection with paranormal studies.

A torsion field is described as a whirlpool or vortex, something ghost hunters claim to have captured in photos as evidence of paranormal energy. The vortex is apparently a tap or connection into time. If this is true, then paranormal energy, in the form of vortices, which give us a view or a vision into the past, can make some sort of sense.

I have seen this vortex in action in an historic farmhouse we were investigating for one of my *Ghosts of Gettysburg* series. Renowned psychic Karyol Kirkpatrick identified it as a "column" of spiritual energy, and when a reporter for the *Gettysburg Times* stood directly in it, her legs began vibrating rapidly. Although she had felt what she called, "static electricity," in an area about eighteen inches around her body, she never felt her legs shaking.[2]

There are other stories in the *Ghosts of Gettysburg* series, which seem to indicate energy emanating from some unknown source in a column or a vortex.

But there is a house on Baltimore Street, within which Time, the Great Arbiter of men's lives, seems to play games via an energy vortex.

The house itself does not date back to the time of the battle. But there was a house there, on that very spot on Baltimore Street. The ancient, hand-dug cellar below the current structure was part of the house that once rested over it. Both the cellar and the house that once stood above it were witnesses to much history and anguish.

First, in the last week of June 1863, raiding Confederates under Jubal Early marched past the original house on the site, through Gettysburg; then, a few days later, Union troops passed, route-stepping bravely into the battle raging in the fields north and west of town. The young women on Baltimore Street sang to them and ran out like maidens in books about knights they'd read, to give their brave defenders flowers, to carry into the coming fight. Within a few hours, some of those same Union troops would come racing back, stumbling through the street, ducking, hiding, trying not to be killed by victorious Rebels chasing after them like hounds after foxes. Past the house then, the Confederates would build a rubble barricade to hide and fight behind. They would occupy Gettysburg for the next three days and roam through the houses at will, "requisitioning" meat, coffee, sugar and canned goods from the owners and paying for it with Confederate script.

They also left a more valuable commodity within the walls of the houses on Baltimore Street: dear comrades, wounded in the fighting, placed in the houses because it was the only shade from the July sun, in the tender care of the women of Gettysburg, who, according to both sides, acted as merciful angels to the wounded and dying in their homes. The dying also apparently left something precious behind as well.

Their souls.

The woman who lived in this particular post-Civil War era house and who related the story is one of Gettysburg's finest business persons. With several stores on Steinwehr Avenue—Habitat, Stoneham's and Camelot Gifts and Souvenirs—she manages them with admirable fastidiousness: all are well-kept, welcoming businesses, catering to the many tourists that visit.

She first moved to Gettysburg about 14 years ago. She'd never had any experiences with ghosts or the paranormal, except for reading the *Ghosts of Gettysburg* book series.

One night in the springtime in her house on Baltimore Street, she was awakened by the familiar chime of a clock. It surprised her because, although she kept a clock on the mantle downstairs, she had never heard it chime before.

A week or so went by. Then, once again, in the middle of the night, the clock chimed. Confused as to why the clock didn't chime during the day on the hour, the woman resolved to investigate the next morning. But with several businesses to run, and a family to care for, by the time she awoke, the matter had slipped her mind.

One evening, she and her family were having dinner. Suddenly, unexpectedly, through the hall and into the dining room echoed the rhythmic, melodious tones: *ding dong ding dong...ding dong ding dong.*

In an interview she related that just below the mantelpiece upon which the clock rested is the old, original, hand-dug cellar from the battle-era house. And while hand-dug cellars, common in many of the older houses in Gettysburg, are no doubt harmless relics of bygone architectural expedience; some feel that with the uneven, packed earth floors they could also be excellent concealers of buried secrets.[3]

The woman herself—remember, a rock-solid business person—admits that it is "very scary" down there in the cellar, and that it is a part of the house she never enters. A week or so before her interview, a man doing a termite inspection went down into the cellar. "I hadn't said anything to him," she said in the interview, "and he came up and said, 'Wow. It's really cold in that basement. It's a strange feeling. Very cold, and it's a hot day.' I proceeded to say 'well, I think that's the old section of the basement and something may have been down there during the war.'

He came up and was quite alarmed at what was going on down there. I never go in there."

Another strange addition to the cellar is a series of large, ancient, wooden shelves or, as she called them, "bunks." "It looks as if there were bunks," she said, "as if soldiers lay there. The bunks are curved as if to hold human bodies."

She has no idea how old the shelves are in the basement, whether they are of the period of the original Civil War era house or not. Her sister-in-law was visiting over one July 4th holiday and she said that she thought that if anyone had been down there and in pain, they might have scratched or marked the wood. She went down into the old cellar. When she came up she had a strange observation: the wood looks as if it had been dug into or clawed at.

The clock that rested on the mantle was made in the state of New York, and the last time she visited the state, she stopped by the manufacturer of the clock. She spoke to the owner of the company and, as she put it in the interview about the chiming clock, "cleared it up completely. He said they don't make chiming clocks. They have no mechanisms to make chiming clocks. And there isn't [a chiming mechanism] if you look at the clock. There's nothing there! If it was just me I would say right, I'm just hearing things. And I don't believe in ghosts!"

She began to keep track of when the chimes were heard. The clock chimed on April 4, 1999. The next time it chimed was again on April 4, 2000. At least four other people besides the woman heard it. "When I've been away, they still recorded on the calendar for me when it chimed. But [it was] not all at the same time. In fact, the young girl who stayed with the house, she's heard it. Actually, she won't stay there anymore."

I asked her how loud was the clock? Is it loud enough to hear in the whole house? "Oh yes. You can hear it upstairs." Could there have been a mistake as to where the chiming was coming from? Perhaps through the wall from a clock next door? Her answer was unequivocal. "You can stand right up to it and it's chiming, right up there."

She seemed to have solved the problem—at least temporarily. "The battery was flat [dead] in the clock. In other words, the clock is not turning around. I took the battery out after the April episode and it hasn't chimed."

But it's not just the clock that gives the sense that there is a conduit—a vortex, if you will—from the old cellar with its mysterious, human-sized shelves, up through the fireplace and the mantle.

"One night," she recalled in the interview, "I'd been cleaning the house and the fireplace has an old cover that you can put on. I think someone was coming to visit the next day. So I felt I better put this cover back on since it usually lies by the fireplace. It was about a quarter to twelve [at night] and I was tired so I made myself a cup of coffee and I sat down and I had a book and thought I'd read for fifteen minutes before going upstairs. And the cover on the fireplace started to rattle. And that really kind of scared me. And I thought that if the cover rattles and the clock goes off, I'm out of here! I'll book a room at the Holiday Inn or something. So I got up and took the cover off straightaway. And I thought, well whatever it is, [it] does not like the cover over that spot. It was right directly under where the clock was. Where the clock was on top, the fireplace was right underneath. It's one of those old, lovely fireplaces with woodwork trim. Since then I've never put the cover back on, I won't have it on. I don't want [it] to rattle in the night."

"Then we've had the doorbell ring. Its an electronic doorbell, it doesn't have batteries, you have to plug it in. One night, the doorbell went and the clock went at the same time. And the doorbell periodically would go, and we'd go to the door and nobody would be there. But that could be some electronic fault?" she asked instead of stated. "The doorbell doesn't work at all now."

Trying to draw some sort of logic to explain the unexplainable, she continued: "But the plug is not far from where the fireplace is. Now I don't have a doorbell anymore. I have a doorbell, but it doesn't work. I'm not saying that's related to the clock. The clock is very weird. It doesn't even have a mechanism to chime with."

The house used to be a bed & breakfast and one woman who had stayed frequently, came in and said, "That place is haunted. Definitely, that house is haunted." She wouldn't relate a specific story, but said only that it was, "just a feeling."

As far as living in the house, with its dirt cellar and body-length, sunken shelves with scratch-marks, and its strange area of energy vortex she said, "I'm okay most of the time, but I know when it gets to midnight, I get up those stairs pretty quickly and close the doors. I know it's an old house and will creak and things like that, but I always have that feeling…."

Finally, in the interview, she was asked what ever happened to the clock?

"Well, I took it out of my house. I had it in the car for weeks and weeks. I drove around with this thing. I don't want the clock going off in the middle of the night. It was on the back seat of the car and never rattled or rang. It only chimes on top of the mantle. I haven't had it on there for a while. I took it off and put it on the chair."

It must be simply a quirk that this one column of physical space that extends from a dank, earthen cellar, up through a fireplace and on up into eternity should remind us, in a most bizarre way, of Time, and his incessant, rhythmic, cadence, drumming each and every one of us who visit Gettysburg, into nothing less than our own oblivion….

The Haunted Clock.

The Substance Of Shadows

Some things have to be believed to be seen.

–Ralph Hodgson

After the savage fighting on the first day at Gettysburg—the Union Army's initial stand west and north of town and the subsequent dissolution of their lines into the town of Gettysburg—the opposing armies formed up in two lines for the most part running north and south on top of two roughly parallel ridges. The Union's Army of the Potomac stretched along the ridge that ran south from the hill the locals had used as their town cemetery to a pair of hills later to be known as Round Top and Little Round Top. The Confederacy's Army of Northern Virginia assembled through the town itself then along a ridge that undulated southward from the Lutheran Seminary. Thus you have the names of the two major terrain features on the Gettysburg Battlefield: Cemetery Ridge and Seminary Ridge.

But they were more than cold "terrain features," or prosaic "battle sites," or tactical "high ground." They were, for two horrid days in American History, Satan's gristmills, grinding men's bodies to bloody bits and flinging off their souls like so much chaff tossed into the wind.

We see, through the dusky glass of our studies, the battle as dispassionate, colored blocks animated in coordinated movements, bumping into one another and recoiling, like some board game in our heads.

And that is good, because if we knew what went on inside those little blocks when they bump together, our deepest, most awful nightmares would suddenly become reality. As the great, dark writer H. P. Lovecraft wrote, "There are horrors beyond horrors, and this was one of those nuclei of all dreamable hideousness which the cosmos saves to blast an accursed and unhappy few." He could have written those words about the

Battle of Gettysburg and its "accursed and unhappy" participants.

Along Seminary Ridge rest a few of what the National Park Service calls "inholdings"—private homes, some historic, some not—islands ensconced within the property the government owns. Needless to say, they are high on the acquisition list.

One is the David McMillan House. It was in existence at the time of the battle, and so, early on the morning of July 1, 1863, Union troops marched past the house on their way to the fighting west of Gettysburg. They were led by the well-respected but doomed Major General John F. Reynolds, who turned down the command of the entire Union Army of the Potomac just days before. He would pass the house again going the other way within just a few minutes, this time an insensible corpse.

Eventually, Seminary Ridge became the main Confederate battleline, and so David McMillan's tidy house, his yards, outbuildings, fields, orchards, and wells, were used by Confederates on July 2, 3 and 4, for water, food, shelter from the sun and rain, for succor after being wounded, and for sepulture after death.

(As a young park ranger, I was riding one of the National Park horses on patrol past the McMillan House when the owner spotted me and rushed over to see the new addition to the park staff—the horse, not me. He was, I discovered, an esteemed professor at Gettysburg College. He called to his wife, a strikingly attractive woman, and offered to hold my horse while she took me on a tour of the historic house. She showed me a bullet hole in one of the doorways and numerous other bits of trivia. In later years, after my first ghost book came out, he graciously approached me. "You want to hear about ghosts?" obviously referring to his home on the battlefield. "Come see me some time. We'll talk.")

Another historic house on Seminary Ridge is "Red Patch," former home of Union Colonel Charles H. T.

Collis. Collis recruited a regiment from Pennsylvania early in the war and had them uniformed in the flamboyant French-styled "zouave" get-up. After their Colonel they would be named "Collis's Zouaves," but officially they would be mustered in as the 114th Pennsylvania Regiment. Colonel Collis is only the second known Medal of Honor recipient buried in the National Cemetery at Gettysburg. The first, of course, is Captain William Miller, 3rd Pennsylvania Cavalry who won the Medal here at Gettysburg for disobeying an order.[1] The difference is that Miller won the Medal for his role at Gettysburg; Collis for action at Fredericksburg, Virginia, December 13, 1862. Near Collis's large tombstone, upon which rests a bronze bust of the Colonel in his youth, are several graves identified as "Unknown Zouave," whose fate their Colonel, mercifully, would not share.

Although buried in the Gettysburg National Cemetery, Colonel Collis did not fight at Gettysburg, being ill during the battle and recovering at his home in Philadelphia. It was probably best, for he may have ended up in the National Cemetery several decades sooner than he did.

You see, his regiment, the 114th Pennsylvania ended up fighting in some of the most vicious combat in the battle, along the Emmitsburg Road, attempting to blunt the virtually unstoppable charge by Barksdale's Mississippians. Their fate in the battle—to be chewed up by what one man called, "the most magnificent charge I witnessed during the war,"[2]—was mild compared to the destiny of some who were merely wounded.

Both Union and Confederate wounded sought shelter in the Sherfy barn, near which they fought. According to a postwar letter to Union General Daniel E. Sickles from Frank E. Moran who became a prisoner of the Confederates, as he was passing the barn, "I could hear the groaning of the wounded within. Shot, shell and bullets had riddled the boards from the ground to the roof."[3] But this was not the worst.

Their groans would soon be replaced by shrieks. While the wounded lay helpless in the barn, it caught fire and burned to the ground, leaving charred, unidentifiable corpses of those helpless, wounded, broken bodies. According to notes gathered by Colonel Jacob M. Sheads, in the Pennsylvania section of the National Cemetery can be found numerous graves marked "Unknown Zouave," referring to Collis's Zouaves, the 114th Pennsylvania Regiment. These graves embrace for eternity the blackened bodies of the wounded who, having survived the combat and holding the hope they might return to their beloved homes and families, died a horrible death in the conflagration of the barn.

So even though he did not participate in the battle, Collis was a soldier, appreciative of great battlefields, and after the war, when it came to settling down, he purchased a parcel right on the most famous battlefield of his war and built a house there. The house must have seemed like a mansion in its day—it seems so now—and he gave it a distinctive name: "Red Patch." His 114th Pennsylvania was part of the Third Corps, 1st Division, whose symbol was a red diamond—a "Red Patch." The name remains to this day.

I remember a story, perhaps apocryphal, from Colonel Sheads. With apologies to any of the Collis clan who may be sensitive to this type of thing, the story has to do with the unique architecture of the house and the nature of Gettysburgians. It seems that Colonel Collis had a back entrance built "below" ground off of West Confederate Avenue. He had an affinity for the ladies and an abhorrence of nosy neighbors. The carriages carrying the "ladies" from Washington, D. C., instead of bouncing through the streets of Gettysburg and up the long hill on Middle Street to "Red Patch," would turn off the Emmitsburg Road at what some locals called "pinch-gut," where Confederate Avenue crosses, and follow West Confederate Avenue to "Red Patch." There the carriages would discreetly turn down behind the house and disgorge their comely passengers into the back entrance. One can almost hear the swishing of silk and rustling of crinolines as the women swept through the elegant home, perhaps to sip champagne and munch on crabmeat brought in from the port of Baltimore, and mingle with other select guest on the spacious front porch of "Red Patch."

One other historic home is the Elizabeth Shultz House that sits upon Seminary Ridge at the corner of Middle Street and West Confederate Avenue. It has most recently been magnificently and faithfully restored by its current residents. And yet, like virtually all the houses in Gettysburg that were here during the battle, it too has its story of death and suffering surrounding it. On the very corner where the Shultz House stands is a stone memorial presented to Co. D, 149th Pennsylvania by George W. Baldwin in memory of his brother, Joseph H. Baldwin, "killed here July 1, 1863" and to Alexander M. Stewart, "mortally wounded and dying in Gettysburg, July 6, 1863." Death, like the unbidden and unwanted relative, overstayed his welcome everywhere in Gettysburg for months after the inferno of combat.

There are two other contemporary houses on the north end of Seminary Ridge. And while the history of their existence does not include the battle fought upon the slopes where they now sit, one of them at least, is replete with unexplainable occurrences and strange visitations.

Suzanne, one of my best friends in Gettysburg approached me, several years after the first ghost book was published, and confessed that she had experienced something of the paranormal when she lived in one of the houses on Seminary Ridge. She prefaced it, however, with a story from a house on York Street and one that predates even that one. Her matter-of-fact accounts of the paranormal experiences in her life amount to an extraordinary chronicle of bizarre, unexplained happenings, both on the Gettysburg Battlefield and off.

She would be the first to admit that she is sensitive to the paranormal. Some of us will admit to a belief, not so much in the paranormal, but in this fact: What we see, hear, taste, touch, and smell is not all there is to this world. It is a concept that is as old as humankind and as widespread. Suzanne's lineage certainly would attest to the fact that she would be more attuned to the spirit world. Somewhere in her distant past is a blood relative that was Native American, a people with a culture that responded directly to insights into the spirit-world. You can see it in her exotic eyes and dark skin, which would tan at the least exposure to the sun; you can see it in her daughters' faces: two lovely young women with the same haunting eyes.

You can also hear the echoes from her Native American ancestors in the telling of her Other Worldly experiences.

The first time she ever saw a spirit was in Easton, Pennsylvania. She was visiting a friend. About ten years before he had dated a woman who had worked in the Playboy Club as one of their famed waitress "bunnies." She was a beautiful, buxom blonde. One evening the man had become deathly ill. The woman found him on the bathroom floor and saved his life. Even though their romantic relationship ended, because of that act of kindness, he always felt close to her. Tragically, she was found murdered in Las Vegas. He got the phone call, asked Suzanne if she would "house sit" for him, and left immediately for the funeral in Nevada.

As Suzanne described it, "I awoke in his house that night and saw a woman standing there—only about two feet away—and I knew it was her. It was just a feeling, but she didn't look at all like her pictures. She had long dark hair; she was really thin and had a sweater over her shoulders."

Suzanne spoke to her but she didn't respond. The "woman" stayed for quite a while, about five minutes, long enough for Suzanne to realize that it wasn't a dream and that she was fully awake. She said she even had time to analyze the apparition and asked herself several questions: "Is it a shadow? Am I misunderstanding this?" But she just stayed very still, standing in one place. "I didn't want to scare her," Suzanne explained, "so I didn't jump out of bed."

The next day her friend came back from Las Vegas. He was sick with remorse. He explained to Suzanne that the former Playboy waitress had gotten into drugs; she was extremely thin; her beautiful blonde hair was long and dark. "I never would have recognized her," he said.

And that was just the way she had appeared to Suzanne in the man's house the night before her funeral. Suzanne's guess is that she returned out of concern. "I think she had loved him and he loved her. I think there was something unfinished there. I don't think she was angry with me; at least I didn't get the feeling of anger. She was just standing in the corner, not far away...."

Suzanne eventually married—but not before dying and coming back from the dead.

But more on that later.

She and her husband lived in Gettysburg on York Street. The building was not standing at the time of the battle: it was a vacant lot owned by Judge Samuel A. Russell in July of 1863. So while the house was not there, the plot of land was, and became witness to and absorber of the bloodletting of some of the vicious street fighting that occurred when Confederates drove Federals through the town on the afternoon of July 1, 1863.

She said there had always been—from the moment they moved in—a certain feeling in the house. *But we all have odd feelings at times in certain circumstances; certainly no reason to move from a house after we've paid the rent and signed a contract. We are reasonable and logical human beings after all, even when confronted with the unknown, unseen and unexplainable...aren't we?*

Everything went fine for a while. They began making friends in Gettysburg and finding their way around. After all, this was just a temporary rental in town while they looked for a "home." But then, one night, she was awakened by that "feeling." As her eyes adjusted and her mind surfaced from the sea of sleep, she saw someone across the room. At first she thought it was her husband, standing there in the middle of the night, oddly looking over the stereo. Her impression was solidified by the fact that he wasn't in bed at that moment. She also saw that the man had a beard—which her husband wore at the time—and thought it was he. She sat up in bed, wondering what he was doing? Sleepwalking? Had the stereo turned on—by itself?—and was he turning it off?

It took her a minute but she slowly began to understand that it wasn't a real human that confronted her, but rather an inhabitant of the World as yet unknown to us. Remember, she had seen a spirit before, and, for better or worse, was familiar with their shape, their demeanor, their "being." She wasn't frightened. In fact she asked, as any good hostess would, "Can I help you?" Apparently, the visitor thought she could because he turned and looked at her. It was then she realized that he wore 19th Century clothing. Unperturbed, she asked again, "Can I help you?" He moved and she saw that he wasn't alone—that a woman was with him dressed in a long, hoop-skirted dress, both wearing clothes seen anymore only in museums—or when the law requires the exhumation of a 19th Century body from the grave. She apparently acknowledged them again, she recalled, either verbally or mentally. Neither answered her but both had turned to look at her, responding to her voice. At that point they just moved—floated, she recalled—across the room and disappeared...through the wall.

In a moment her husband entered the room. He had been downstairs getting a drink of water.

A later renter of the house, a woman whom Suzanne had known before, approached her and said she had a strange question to ask. She asked her if she'd ever had any experiences with spirits in the house. Suzanne asked her what made her think there were spirits there. "My daughter keeps talking about a man, mainly in the kitchen area. She keeps saying, 'Mommy, there's that man again.' Of course, I can't see anything even when she says she's pointing at him."

Suzanne and her family—there were two young daughters now—moved to one of the "inholdings" on West Confederate Avenue. It was there that they met "T.J."

Her youngest daughter was a little past two-years-old. She and her older sister shared a front room as their bedroom. The younger sister's bed was near a staircase that had been closed off because the upstairs was rented to tenants. She would tell her mother about the man who would visit her in her room—a kindly, protective, older man who would come down the stairs into her room...even though they had been blocked off by a sealed wooden door. She never saw him, but knew he was there, felt his presence like a stranger behind her back in the room.

Occasionally she would wake in the middle of the night and say there was a man standing by her bed. When asked about the man later, when she was in her late teens, she said that she never felt threatened by his presence; it was always a good feeling, and that she felt he was "a protector of the house." She felt the presence of the man from the time she was about two years old until she was about six.

When the family got a pet, the dog would act strangely at certain times, staring at the closed-up stairway, moving its gaze slowly from one side of the room to the other, obviously noticing someone or something moving past but invisible to everyone else in the room.

One day they re-arranged the furniture in the girl's room. When they moved the bed away from the stairs, as if he felt no longer needed, he never appeared to the little girl again.

During one of our many conversations, Suzanne and I discovered that we had mutual friends in a married couple—two of the first people I met when I first moved to Gettysburg.

Lynn and her husband graduated from Gettysburg College. I always remembered her as one of the more mature, down-to-earth people living in Gettysburg over that first remarkable summer I spent here. So I wasn't surprised years later when we ran into each other again, that she had been working at one of the more prestigious physics institutes in the nation. Her choice of work certainly reflected her skeptical, logical and thoughtful approach to things.

Lynn was helping Suzanne at a party at Suzanne's house. She was bringing some drinks from the front porch, down the hall. Suzanne said that she saw her pass a door to a closet built under the stairs to the second floor, move out of the way and say, "Oh, excuse me." She brought the drinks to the end of the hall and Suzanne smilingly said, "What was *that* little movement?"

"Well, the guy in the tweed jacket just came out of the closet and I almost ran into him."

"What guy?" Suzanne asked. She had seen nothing except the odd dodge Lynn had made at the empty doorway.

"I almost ran into that guy in the jacket. He almost made me spill the drinks."

Suzanne had a difficult time explaining that there had been no man in a tweed jacket at the door; there was no one by that description at the party. And, in fact, he was never seen again…at least not at *that* gathering.

From that day, everyone began calling him T. J.—for "tweed jacket." The girls would often talk to him, especially the youngest. As with the first spirit they encountered at Gettysburg, there was always a feeling of kindness and protectiveness surrounding their experience with T. J. As the youngest would say, " T. J.'s watching over us."

A couple of years later, a relative was visiting who had never heard the story of T. J. She and Suzanne were having a serious talk on the porch. But she kept being distracted, looking over Suzanne's shoulder, and finally apologized: "I'm sorry. I keep seeing this guy with a tweed jacket standing behind you. I see him, then I don't see him; I see him, then I don't."

When Suzanne first told me that she lived on West Confederate Avenue, I thought that she might have lived in the famous Red Patch, but she said no.

I asked her if she knew anything about the house. She replied that she knew it had an historic sign in front of it, and so it must have had something to do with the battle. Beyond that, she knew nothing. I enjoyed re-telling the story of Colonel Collis and his clandestine parties and the arrival of women in their finery to partake of the Colonel's hospitality.

She got a funny look in her eye. "Maybe that explains it." She proceeded to tell me a story of a vision into the past.

One night, her girls were having a sleepover with their young friends and neighbors. One of the little girls who lived in Red Patch had forgotten her sleeping bag and was going to walk to get it. Suzanne stood on the porch of her house to watch over her. As she waited, she suddenly got a strange feeling, as she put it, "a feeling when you're in another space, another time. It was almost like I was the one in the wrong place.

"There was a scene on the porch at Red Patch. It was all couples, talking directly to each other, four or five couples. It felt like I was in another time. The women wore long dresses, perhaps from the turn of the century. The men in early 1900s-style tails and bowties. They looked almost Victorian, very fancy dresses, and definitely not a working class of people."

She said the vision didn't last long, 45 seconds at the most, but long enough to see them chatting, laughing, sipping champagne, and clinking glasses in a toast, perhaps to the late war and its heroes, before the entire scene vanished before her eyes.

"It felt like they didn't know that I was there and I was in their space rather than me being there and them being in my space." It is understandable why she would feel that way: Their "space" of course, was not only fifty yards away, but some eight or nine decades previous to hers.

However, as strange as that vision may seem, there is something even more bizarre to the tale. All those experiences—the Victorian cocktail party, "T.J." the man and the woman apparitions on York Street, the vision of the dead Playboy Bunny, and everything else she's experienced since—occurred at a unique period in her life.

They all happened after she died.

She was 27 when she had a car accident on the Schuylkill Expressway. Anyone who has traveled that stretch of highway outside of Philadelphia, especially in the 1970s, will remember the name the locals gave it: The Sure-kill Expressway. In her case, it was prophetic. What happened after the crash, which was as horrific as anyone can imagine, is best told in her words:

"I was out of my body. [I only remember that] I got hurt and at that moment I felt this great, incredible lifting feeling. Like when you dream you're flying. You stay horizontal and just lift up. Then there seemed to be some kind of..." She paused to collect her thoughts and gather in her emotions. It is unsettling to recall one's own death.

She continued speaking of her visit to the Netherworld: "My grandfather was there and my mother's mother who died when my mother was two years old. So I didn't know her. [There were] two others there that I did not know. They seemed to be in a little different realm. They were straight across from me—not above me—and close, but there still seemed to be some kind of unseen, different space. That's when I said to my self, 'Oh this is death. I'm dead. This is death.'"

She paused and corrected herself. "But I couldn't even think that word because there was absolutely no death. People don't understand me unless I use that word when I try and describe the experience, so I'm using that word. But that's not what you'd even call it, but I know in my head, 'oh that's what this is about.' Then I was given a choice—it feels like it was a choice—about going back to my body. I was aware I wasn't in my body but I was so comfortable that I wasn't like looking down and going...."

She paused to try to reconstruct in words something that goes beyond mere words.

"So I don't know if I was directed this, I felt like I said it. I was able to say, 'Hi grandpa!' And he goes, 'Everything's okay,' but there was no talking. Everything was all done mentally."

Her next comments were as prophetic as they are revealing:

"The reason I went back to my body is because I had to let people know that we don't die, and I hadn't loved everyone I needed to love. Those were the two reasons, but I don't know if they were ordained reasons or my decision reasons. And just like that in making that decision, I went back to my body, I woke up on the road, they were working on me and I was like, 'Don't cut off this jumpsuit, I just bought it, I paid so much for it at Wanamakers.' They were worried about my leg, not knowing I had a totally crushed chest. It was totally concave. Every rib broken away from the sternum. Everybody dies from the injuries I sustained. But I kept talking. They say because I kept talking I lived."

She endured eight hours of surgery. Her parents and brother flew out from the Midwest. The doctors, for a while, thought she had jaundice. She was on a respirator and was virtually paralyzed.

"When they came in I could move my finger and I knew that I had to let them know I was okay. I was able to just barely lift up my finger. My brother saw it and said, 'she's going to be okay.'"

And, as with all such things, there are a couple of synchronicities, one directly associated with Gettysburg.

It was about two or three years after the accident, when she was living in the York Street house. She and her husband were selling a pump organ. A man entered the house to look at it, sat down and started playing "Jesus loves me" and "Rock of Ages." He appeared to be enjoying himself immensely. Suddenly he looked up at Suzanne and said, "I know you somehow." She told him her name. She recounted what happened next: "He leapt from the organ stool and picked me up and said, 'I can't believe you're alive. I prayed over you for a week.'" He had been at the seminary and had an internship at the Philadelphia Hospital. His last week at the seminary was her first week in the hospital after the accident. He left assuming, because of the severe nature of her injuries, she had died.

"When my body decided to get better it was overnight," she recalled. "I'll never forget the night it happened. They didn't know if I was going to live one night, and the next day I was up walking. I'd been on the respirator for a month then they took me off. I was discharged directly from intensive care." The doctors had planned for her to be in the hospital another two months.

A priest who had been praying for her daily wrote a letter to her hometown paper entitled "I Witnessed a Miracle."

In the interview I asked her, To what do you attribute your recovery? There was a very long pause. "I think it *was* a miracle," she finally said. "I was really cared about here. People sent their prayers, or sent energy...."

Since her death...and rebirth on that Philadelphia expressway, she has always delved into the more mysterious and fascinating aspects of life—both this life and the next...and perhaps the previous ones also. She has studied "chakras" or the energy concentrations in the body. She often talked, when having a bad day, about her chakras being out of line. Suzanne used to meditate regularly. One day she meditated so deeply, she missed going to work.

That day she got a phone call from a friend who said, "You saved my life today. I was driving and you were right in the car with me and you told me exactly what to do." Her friend avoided a potentially deadly accident.

Some paranormal researchers call this an "O. B. E."—out-of-body experience—or teleportation. It has happened several times to her.

There is another experience this remarkable woman shared with me. I don't want to say "final," experience because the story of her life, in spite of Death's best efforts, thankfully, isn't over yet. It too is a story of energy. It is a story of how the greatest force in this world is not atomic power or the ultimate, vast energy of the cosmos, but an unseen energy, one that cannot be measured or calculated by instruments, or analyzed by scientists. Its existence is instead confirmed by a feeling, and that, like the paranormal, flies in the face of the scientific method. This energy disregards Newton's and Einstein's laws of physics, and pushes beyond time and space, and exists in a realm all its own, much like the soul apparently does.

It is the energy of love.

Suzanne is originally from the heartland of America. She was the quintessential Midwestern girl: raised on her father's farm, high school cheerleader, dating the hometown boyfriend. She might have married him too, if war, like it has so often over the millennia, hadn't gotten in the way.

His strong convictions and devout patriotism drew him to volunteer to fight in what may have been America's second most controversial war (the Civil War, of course, being the most controversial since it literally tore the country in half.) He went to Vietnam. She drifted away: off to college, a job in the east, another man, a husband, children, another life in Gettysburg, Pennsylvania. Then a divorce, a new house, the always-unique "dating scene."

Then she ran into him again. As fate would have it, they rekindled the affections they'd held inside for nearly thirty years and were married.

With two daughters in college in the east, she returned to Gettysburg fairly frequently. He is a very successful businessman, and couldn't travel with her each time. Nevertheless, at least one memorable night, in spite of 1200 miles of separation, they were together.

Upon returning to him from a trip to Gettysburg, she heard her husband—a down-to-earth, no-nonsense, entrepreneur-type—tell her of a strange, nighttime encounter.

"You were here with me," he said. "The other night when you were in Gettysburg. I felt you right next to me. Your energy was here, in our room."

Telling me the story, she took a philosophical, practical, even humorous attitude about her ability to teleport: "I wonder if that happens a lot and people just don't share it with me." She laughed. "No wonder I wake up tired—I'm off visiting other people all night!".

Translucent Reality

Visual information entering our brains is edited and modified by our temporal lobes before it is passed on to our visual cortices. Some studies suggest that less than 50 percent of what we 'see' is actually based on information entering our eyes.

–Michael Talbot,
The Holographic Universe

Culp's Hill was the scene of some of the longest, most intense, and most horrifying of all the fighting at Gettysburg. An initial Confederate assault on the Union lines there began late in the evening of July 2. Confederates in Johnson's Division, starting from their positions on the Daniel Lady Farm on the Hanover Road, found the going tougher than they expected: Rock Creek was a serious impediment as the Rebels were peppered by stubborn Yankee skirmishers as they crossed; the terrain on that side of the hill was, in some places, precipitous cliffs fifteen to twenty feet high; the Yankees had cleared fields of fire and built formidable breastworks; and worst of all, darkness had fallen and they were virtually groping in the dark, firing at musket flashes, never being able to identify them as friend or foe.

As it was, they almost met with incredible success. Their opponent, Union Brigadier General George S. Greene—63-years-old at the time of the battle—was forced to spread his 1400 men dangerously thin along the breastworks. In fact, during the attack, Confederates actually gained possession of the right of the Union works and were within a few minutes march of the Baltimore Pike and the rear of the Union line.

As one Union participant put it: "The left of our brigade was only about eighty rods [one-quarter of a mile] from the Baltimore turnpike, while the right was somewhat nearer. There were no supports. All the force that there was to stay the onset was that one thin line. Had the breastworks not been built, and had there been only the thin line of our unprotected brigade, that line must have been swept away like leaves before the wind."[1]

The fighting would die down late at night on July 2, only to start up again as soon as it was light enough on July 3, and last until about 11:00 A.M.—some of the longest continuous fighting during the three days of battle. When it was over, the dead and dying were scattered about.

When wounded, the first thing men usually cry for is water. With the battle having been fought in the heat of July, the nervousness of going into battle, and the immediate dehydration a wound brings, they were deathly thirsty. As the realization settled in that they were hurt badly, some—officers particularly—would ask those around them to pass on a message to loved ones back home: "Tell Father I died with my face to the foe," was typical. If alone, they'd call for help so that comrades, or even the enemy, might find them. Some, even the older soldiers, as they died, regressing to their first childhood memories, would be heard crying like children for their mothers.

Their cries for help, for water, for their comrades, for their mothers, were pitiful and unnerving. Long throughout the night of July 2 and even into the dark morning of July 3, men continued their heart-rending pleas that could be heard echoing everywhere in the darkened and forbidding woods of Culp's Hill: *Water...Help...Help me...Water...Mother...Oh, God....*

In December 2001, I received a letter from an M.D. who admitted having been attracted to the battlefield of Gettysburg since he was 4-years-old. (This is not uncommon in serious battlefield buffs and historians. William Frassanito, esteemed Gettysburg scholar and author recalls his first fascination with Gettysburg began at age eight; I too was enchanted by the fabled name "Gettysburg" when I was only seven. Some go so far as to hint that this early attraction stems from a "past-life" experience at Gettysburg. Reenactors in particular, often feel this way…).

In 1987, the doctor and his family and a friend were staying at the old "Welcome Traveler" Campground on the Baltimore Pike. Spangler's Spring and Culp's Hill are only a hundred or so yards from the campground. He recalled that it was the first week in July, the week of the 124th Anniversary of the battle. One night, they had gathered around their nightly campfire to relax and talk. It was about 11:15 P.M. He had gone into the trailer when he was called back out by his family. All they said was, "Listen."

From the dank, darkened woods of Culp's Hill, once carpeted with the horribly mangled victims of our national fratricide, echoed a pitiful and disturbing cry:

Help me….

They stood in shocked silence. A minute passed. Then, again, rising mournfully from the woods:

Help…me…. Then silence.

He was just about to relegate it to the collective active imaginations of the family. But then, once more, emerging from the darkness of that shadowed hill it came:

Help…me….

And, as they stood disbelieving, twice more the agonized pleading rolled from the woods: *Help…me….Help…me….*

The doctor reasoned that someone must have gone out on the battlefield after dark illegally, perhaps with a metal detector, had fallen and was lying helpless. As a doctor, his first instinct was to help. He got the campsite owner. As they strained their ears toward the distant, grim woods, it came again, pleading,

Help…me….

Although the National Park is closed after 10:00 P.M., they realized that this might be an emergency. They got into the camp owner's car and rushed up the road that led from the Baltimore Pike to Culp's Hill. They passed Spangler's Spring and proceeded several hundred feet up the hill towards the summit of Culp's Hill. They stopped the car and turned it off. There, from the woods just a few hundred feet ahead and above them on the hill, the voice: *Help...me....*

On up the slope they drove, stopped the car again, shut it off and listened. There, just ahead of them, the anguished cry: *Help...help...me....*

And so it went. Again and again the pleading, *Help...me....* Always, just a few yards ahead of them, the wretched cry: *Help...help...me....*

Several times they stopped the car when they were certain the voice was just inside the woods that edge the road, and got out into the lowering darkness. Just when they thought they were heading in the right direction, when they thought they were right on top of it, a voice would be heard in another direction. Always, the haunting appeal, *Help...me....*

They continued their methodical but frustrating search along the onyx hillside for about 35 to 40 minutes, always thinking they were just about to stumble over the injured person, only to hear the voice, a few yards in the distance. It was as if someone were purposefully leading them deeper and deeper into the Culp's Hill woods.

One can only stay on the battlefield after it is closed for a short time before the inevitable occurs. They soon saw the flashing red and blue lights of a Park Ranger vehicle. The ranger got out of his patrol car and asked them what they were doing there after the park had closed. They explained to the skeptical ranger who was, no doubt, prepared to write them a ticket. "Just listen," they asked.

Two or three minutes had gone by. The ranger's patience was wearing thin. Then, as before, from the oppressive woods in the distance, the pitiful, tormented cry: *Help...me....*

Convinced now that there might be someone accidentally injured on the hill where once hundreds were purposefully hurt by their fellow men, the ranger radioed for assistance. Soon, another ranger came to help find the apparently injured man, or perhaps several injured men, since the cry seemed to come from so many places.

Again, as the four stood there on the darkened hillside, came the cry for assistance. Again the pinpointing of the location, now by four sets of ears and the powerful flashlights of the rangers. And again his location not found. And again the call from somewhere else up on the hill. For a while it must have seemed as if there was not one man injured on Culp's Hill that night, but scores.

Finally, at about 1:30 A.M., the search was called off. As they walked to their cars, the mournful wails faded behind them, as if mocking their efforts. They returned to the campground. All were frustrated and agreed that even though they had scoured the hill, the voice—or voices—were unable to be located. It was as if there were too many to find, too many to help. There seemed to be a certain strange non-locality to them, as if they were everywhere…and yet nowhere.

The doctor asked the rangers what the next step was. They responded that it was just another unknown they would put into the log.

The next day the doctor and his party went back to the site where they had heard the cries so vivid and so numerous the night before. There was nothing. No tracks, other than their own, at the several spots where the doctor, the campground owner, and the rangers had investigated, the spots where they were convinced they had surrounded the injured man, only to be called off in another direction by another cry for help.

Part of the reason paranormal encounters often go unreported is because the common inquiry is "Have you ever seen a ghost?" Honest people will usually have to admit, no, they've never seen a ghost, and so they themselves figure they haven't had a true paranormal experience. But that doesn't mean they haven't had a paranormal experience. According to researchers, only about 10–11 percent of all paranormal experiences are visual; a good 60 percent are auditory, and the rest are spread out between tactile, olfactory, and just plain odd, unexplainable feelings. You don't have to see a ghost to have one present, and yet the most eerie, most unexplainable, and often the most frightening reports are of the sighting of a spirit entity….

A letter I received from a military historian for the Kentucky National Guard caught my attention, first because of the source. Historians I consider to be very skeptical professionals who are some of the last to believe in the paranormal events occurring on a battlefield where some of the documented events are frightening enough. And secondly, because the story he told was of the rare version of paranormal encounters: the actual sighting of an apparition.

On July 7, 2000—again around the anniversary of the battle—he brought his family to Gettysburg. They took one of the Licensed Battlefield Guided Tours then walked the battlefield in chronological order to understand the fighting a little better. They purchased the *Ghosts of Gettysburg* books and took a tour with *Ghosts of Gettysburg Candlelight Walking Tours*®. On the second day of their visit they toured the Culp's Hill area. They noticed the marker for the 66th Ohio Infantry that fought upon the slopes and a path leading to the monument where Major Joshua Palmer was killed.

The battle of Gettysburg had raged for two days now. On the morning of July 3, it was still dark when Major Palmer and the men of the 66th were ordered over the crest of Culp's Hill and told to place themselves perpendicular to the rest of the Union line. Even the general officer in charge was incredulous, telling the commander of the 66th that the enemy was right upon them and would "simply swallow" the regiment if they went out to their assigned position. Yet the men from the Buckeye State moved themselves into harm's way. Immediately they were fired upon; immediately they took casualties, but managed to drive the Virginians who were before them. Throughout the morning they held, perhaps because of the courageous example of a small-town dentist who apparently turned down the safety of a rear-echelon medical corps position for the oak leafed shoulder boards of a line officer. Major Joshua G. Palmer of Urbana, Ohio, was mortally wounded and fell and bled out his life near a large rock on the side of the hill. If he had been a good dentist, he must have been a far better soldier for there is a monument to him placed on the rock that commemorates his mortal wounding on the field of battle.[2]

Path to the Marker for Major Palmer.

At 8:30 P.M. the historian and his family returned to Culp's Hill. They were disappointed to see that someone was on the tower, and so decided to go down into the woods to visit the Ohio monument again.

As they descended the hill, the virtually impenetrable woods on Culp's Hill closed in on them creating an eerie, oppressive darkness, much like that experienced by struggling Confederate troops who assaulted the well-defended Union positions at the summit of Culp's Hill then were driven back down the hill into the murk of the woods and oncoming night.

No doubt as they descended into the darkness they trod on spots where brave men bled their last, dying, screaming in agony or silent as lambs, calmly awaiting the transmigration of their soul, or fearfully dreading their encounter with either their Benevolent Creator or the Great Imposter, whichever their lives would compel them to spend eternity with.

About halfway down the path, the military historian was disappointed again at seeing someone standing at the bottom of the hill looking at the dead Ohio Major's marker. Peering into the growing darkness, his wife saw the vague shadow of a man as well. The man took his two children by the hand and stepped off to the side of the narrow trail as his wife stepped to the other side, to allow room for the stranger to pass.

They waited a few moments, but as no one passed, they looked back down the trail. The man was still standing, staring eerily at the marker, but now appeared merely as the ill-defined, fuzzy outline of a man. The historian blamed the fading vision on the failing light, yet one is compelled to think perhaps something else was at work. As the historian wrote, "It was obviously a man because of the large size, and he appeared to be wearing a Civil War fashion forage cap." This came as no surprise since he knew the caps were sold locally and that there were a number of reenactors about the battlefield. The family decided to continue down the path even though someone was there.

As they started down the hill, the individual turned to face them. Again they started to step aside to allow him to pass, but as they did, the historian witnessed the impossible: the figure simply vanished, fading like a wisp into the eerie Otherworldliness of that once horrid hillside. Shocked, but attempting to reason out the disappearance, he tried to rationalize that the man had just gone down the trail. As they continued the few steps to the Major's death marker, the historian was surprised when he felt the temperature drop at least 20 to 25 degrees. While his family looked at the marker, the historian attempted to find the man in the Civil War kepi that seemed to have vanished. He began to follow the pathway down the hill but realized that the woods opened up just a few feet from the Major's marker. Anyone moving down the hill would have been seen. He looked in all directions, but saw no one.

When he returned to the marker, his children had in their hands a fresh white rose that they had found lying at the foot of the marker. It had not been there a couple of hours before when they visited. His wife said nothing about the hazy, indistinct form of a soldier who was there, then was not there.

They paid their respects to the fallen officer and began to ascend the hill to the parking area. As they did the temperature rose rapidly. They visited the tower, took some pictures, and his wife remembered that she hadn't taken a snapshot of the Major's memorial. As they hurried back down the hill to the marker, the historian expected to feel the cold of the woods cloak them again. Instead, as they descended, the temperature grew hotter and the humidity became foul and choking. By the time they reached the marker, they were all sweating profusely, when just moments before they had shivered in a dry, icy, unnatural cold.

On their drive back to the hotel, his wife hesitantly inquired, when he noticed the soldier at the bottom of the hill, if he seemed to just disappear. When her husband answered in the affirmative, it was then he found out that his wife had experienced the same things he had: the icy cold, then the humid heat, and, of course, the soldier who simply dematerialized before their eyes.

One is left to ponder this: Was the apparition one of Major Palmer's loyal men making sure no one had defiled the monument to courage, tenacity and sacrifice made to hold the rocky hillside?

Or could it have been the Major, himself, standing there again, questioning the decision he once made to leave the comfortable, mundane world of repairing people's teeth, to unknowingly seek the early death he found when the rock-strewn slope of Culp's Hill became his personal dying-place?

George Armstrong Custer was one of the heroes of the Battle of Gettysburg. Thirteen years later he was on the way to a fated rendezvous with his end at a creek called the Little Big Horn. One of his Crow scouts, like the other Native American scouts who rode with Custer, had a fearful premonition of what lay ahead. "You and I," he told Custer, "are both going home today by a road that we do not know."³ It is a road the soldier on Culp's Hill traveled at one time...and is apparently still traveling. It is a lonesome—and common—road we all are doomed to travel...sooner or later.

When Heaven and Hell Changed Places

*What is so strange or unusual about dying? You just walk back
out the same door you came in. When you came in you had no
complaints about where you'd come from.*

–General George S. Patton

All soldiers, from the very beginning of armies and
warfare, have fought two foes. First, they battle the sworn
enemy of their country, who, if the Gods of battle smile
upon them that particular day, they may defeat. But they
also fight the one merciless, tireless, aggressive adversary,
against whom every soldier ever born fights: Death, who
marches into the fray in legions. Death, of course,
inevitably wins all in the end.

And it must have looked like Death's Legions to the
Union soldiers lined up on Cemetery Ridge at 3:00 P.M.,
July 3, 1863, as 12,500 Confederates emerged from the
woods on Seminary Ridge. Methodically they began their
slow march, gradually emerging from the woods, more and
more of them every second, until they practically filled the
entire, broad width of the farm fields before them.

Had the men on Cemetery Ridge been able to look just
an hour into the future, they would have seen that very
plain covered with a vast red carpet of dead and wounded,
so many struggling to rise in vain or waving broken and
torn limbs, that the field would take on, as one observer put
it, "a singular crawling effect." Captain George Bowen
from the 12th New Jersey recalled that, "the dead and
wounded lay as thick as one ever saw sheaves of wheat in a
harvest field, for a distance of a hundred yards or more in
front and as far to the right and left as the eye can reach."

Once it became dark and safe to venture out into the
killing field, Bowen took his canteen out among the wounded
enemy, attempting to relieve some of their suffering. When it
was empty, he found some water in a ditch beside the

Emmitsburg Road. Even in the dark he could see the road and the ditch were filled with Confederate dead. He gave some water to the nearest wounded man who asked him if he could find some other water. "This is so full of blood I cannot drink it," he said.[1]

And if they'd been able to look even farther into the future, they probably would not have even recognized the killing fields across which they and their enemies had struggled and bled and died.

Shortly after the carnage of Longstreet's Assault on July 3, 1863, burials scarred the land between the Bryan Farm, the Codori Farm and the fields west of the Emmitsburg Road. Within a few months the Union graves would be opened by the score and the bodies ripped from their sepulture, as if it were the Great Day of Resurrection. But instead of confronting their Judge, they were carted a few hundred yards to the newly purchased National Cemetery and re-buried where they now rest awaiting the true Judgment Day.

It wouldn't be until the 1870s that the hundreds of Confederate graves, which pocked the vast areas both west and east of the Emmitsburg Road, would be opened and the sons of the South sent home—often packed several to the crate—to various cemeteries in the larger Southern cities.

By the time of the Twenty-fifth Anniversary of the battle in 1888, some monuments were beginning to dot the landscape, most placed there by the veterans themselves or the War Department (as the Department of Defense was called back then) to indicate troop positions during the battle. As visitation to Gettysburg grew, roads were cut by wagons carrying the curious and their guides—mostly knowledgeable townsfolk—to the most popular (usually the most bloody) sites. Later these roads were paved.

In 1895, Congress legislated into existence Gettysburg National Military Park. Shortly thereafter, as if the fields of Gettysburg were forever meant for war, the U. S. Army, during the Great War, constructed a tank training camp known as Camp Colt under the direction of Dwight D. Eisenhower. With roaring, treaded machines cutting swaths across the terrain, and the new officers' swimming pool dug in the middle of the real estate where Civil War soldiers were wounded and killed, the field of Pickett's Charge would have been hardly recognizable to the old soldiers. It was about that time the veterans returned for the Fiftieth Anniversary of the battle in 1913, and so they could appreciate the changes wrought by man and time.

The ensuing years brought more changes: with the Great Depression came Civilian Conservation Corps members who rebuilt stone walls that had crumbled and replaced post and rail and Virginia worm wood fences that had disappeared since the battle. This, then, answers the question so many visitors ask: "Are the fences original?" More new roads were added to the park.

In the 1950s vacations became the pastime of not just the rich, but of all social classes, and Gettysburg became a destination. Motels with restaurants and swimming pools sprouted along Steinwehr Avenue, some being built on ground over which some of Longstreet's men trod on their forced march to Eternity.

One must wonder what the men of the Army of Northern Virginia—as Joshua Chamberlain had called it, "that great army which ours had been created to confront for all that death can do for life"—and the men of the Army of the Potomac—"an army of tested manhood, clothed with power, crowned with glory…"—what they would feel and think about their battlefield—for it is indeed not ours but theirs, purchased with their pain and suffering—and how they would react to its ever-changing countenance, altered by businessmen and superintendents alike.

From its blood-soaked appearance when they first saw it, to today, it seems assured they would hardly recognize it.

A young woman from a nearby college comes to the National Military Park at Gettysburg often for the sheer beauty the area provides. She will watch the sunset on Little Round Top, or spend time in Devil's Den, awestruck by the incredible geologic power the massive boulders represent. She often brings friends to the fields as well. And while basking in the natural beauty all around them, occasionally they will be reminded, by supernatural means, of the anachronism represented by the now lush fields, once splattered with the gore of 51,000 men and boys.

It was Labor Day weekend and the temperature was still very warm from the bright, sunny day. She and several friends from a sports team were visiting Gettysburg for the evening. They first went to Devil's Den, walked around the area for a little while, then returned to their car and drove down Cemetery Ridge until they reached the legendary High Water Mark—the allegorical "High Tide" of the Confederacy, where Longstreet's Assault (more popularly known as Pickett's Charge) wasted itself in a maelstrom of blood and broken dreams.

The sun had set about a half hour before, and so the young ladies exited their car with some apprehension. They had prior knowledge of the area into which they walked, of the brave men—about their age—who found themselves engulfed in the mortal terror of sudden death. If they had forgotten, there would be plenty to remind them in the next few minutes.

First, as they approached the famous stone wall behind which the Federal Army's Second Corps waited for Longstreet's men, they saw, silhouetted in what little light there was left, the monument to the men of the 69th Pennsylvania Volunteers upon which is a bronze statue with musket reversed, held high over its head like a baseball bat, about to bring it down upon the form of a now, long dead Confederate foe. This to show how primitive was the fight that raged at this point in the battle.

As they approached the area where some three hundred Confederates following Brigadier General Lewis A.

Armistead temporarily broke through the Union line only to be beaten, clubbed, shot, gutted, or brained with rocks and physically thrown back, the women suddenly passed through a huge area of freezing cold on this warm, early-September night. It was so suddenly intense, so ominous, so cold that two of them went running back to the car, frightened nearly to death. Three others, though shaken by the experience, decided to continue through the site of carnage where Southern hopes for independence evaporated.

Chain at the High Water Mark.

They got to a row of granite blocks—monuments to the individual companies of the 69th Pennsylvania—connected by massive black chains. For a while these had been removed from the battlefield and put in storage by the National Park Service, but, within the last ten years, had been resurrected and placed presumably in the same spots the veterans originally identified as their positions.

The chains hang separately between each granite post. As the three women approached, they realized that one of the huge chains was swinging. As they were alone in the area their first thought was that the wind had moved the chain so smoothly, almost, the woman wrote, "like a hand was guiding it." But its sheer mass belied the fact: it would have taken a hurricane to move that chain.

One of the other women moved to another chain and touched it. Holding it in her hand for a few seconds, she suddenly jumped back, startling the others. "It's vibrating," she announced, and sent the rest of them running toward the car.

Halfway to the car they stopped and allowed reason and common sense to return. After all, this was just another field, just another stone wall and a few monuments, right? They decided to investigate their friend's claim.

They returned to the chain that, by now, had stopped swinging. The author of the letter picked the chain up to see if the wind could actually make it swing, but it was far too heavy to be moved in any light breeze they had felt that warm summer night. She swung the chain to see if she could replicate the movement with the human hand. Of course, like any chain hung between two solid objects, when touched at a spot, it begins a wave-like motion. So it was with the chain she touched: a wave-like, "choppy" motion, far removed from the smooth, swinging motion the entire chain displayed when they first approached it. One person could not have moved the chain as it moved; it would have taken—well, there's no other way to put it—an entire company of men to swing it like a solid piece of metal.

One other thing she noticed: in spite of the hot day, and still warm evening, and the fact that the metal was painted a heat-absorbing black, the chain, to her touch, was icy cold.

One final experience this woman and a friend had the next summer while walking the fields through which Pickett's, Pettigrew's, and Trimble's men advanced on their march to mutual immolation, impressed her enough to write about it. It echoes an experience some reenactors had while acting the part of the fated men during the filming of the movie "Gettysburg."

It was 1997 and a hot day. They walked out into the farm fields, shimmering with the heat, past the National Park Service orientation maps and audio stations, and out onto the ground to about where the Confederates first began to feel the mortal sting of Federal artillery. Up the slight rises and down again into the troughs in the land they strode, attempting to re-live the last walk of so many brave souls, born in the South, only to die here at Gettysburg. Suddenly, they hit a wall of freezing cold. There, in that sweltering field, they could see their breath condense in the chill. Cold air? Not likely. But perhaps something else. It has happened before to others....

*　　*　　*

In August 1996, a woman and her husband were taking a stroll at dusk, just as things were beginning to cool off. They sat at the benches near the Copse of Trees—descendants of the trees Confederate General Robert E. Lee pointed to and told Pickett's men to aim for—when they began to smell wood smoke: the smell that accompanies modern wood fires, but also the odor of the hundreds of fires built by the soldiers in the area...thirteen decades past. The problem is that the Copse of Trees is virtually in the middle of the National Park where no open fires are allowed, and while some of the historic houses have fireplaces, most are closed off for the safety of the irreplaceable structures. Not to mention the fact that, in the heat of summer, who would build a fire in a fireplace?

They began to walk across the area towards the right of the Copse of Trees, through the small space where Armistead's men broke the Union line and were hurled back by the Federals in vicious hand-to-hand fighting. Men died virtually anywhere you set foot in that space. As they walked, suddenly they would pass through what she described as "hot spots," places where you could actually feel heat energy coming up from the ground in a column. Curious, they walked around and found dozens more.

It was almost completely dark now. Looking back at the Copse of Trees from the area near "The Angle" they suddenly saw, from off to the left, four or five bright flashes of light, not all at once like a volley, but more like "firing at will." They thought about it and determined, by the singularity and grouping of the flashes, they could not be cameras going off. After their other experiences in the area, they began to feel frightened and left.

Another couple, in June 1996, was visiting "The Angle" about 9:45 P.M., just before the park closed. They had just parked their car near the low stone wall when the husband said, "What are those white things?" and pointed to the left. His wife looked and said that she thought they were the wheels to the cannon that stood there. Her husband informed her that the cannon wheels are dark-colored, not white. She looked again and the thin white lines had grown into two white figures, one on either side of the cannon. She described what she saw: "They both had no features, no shadows or lights, but I could see 2 heads, necks, shoulders, upper torsos, pants and legs slightly open." She went on to write that the figure on the left had his arm stretched out and up a little, and could have moved slightly.

Human-like figures that morph from thin wisps of mist into heads, necks, torsos, legs and arms that move? Half visible and half transparent realm; half real and half counterfeit souls; oh, what strange kind of world is this we inhabit, all of us, beings and non-beings, one and all?

I received a letter from a man who visited Gettysburg with his family. He began his letter like this: "On July 3, 1994, while vacationing in Gettysburg with my family, an incident occurred which we believe introduced us to the other world that Gettysburg lies in."

They had visited the marker dedicated to Brigadier General Lewis Armistead at "The Angle" earlier in the day and had returned to the area after dinner. They spoke a few minutes with some other visitors who soon left the site. Off on the horizon a thunderstorm began rolling in, crossing the valley between the South Mountains and Gettysburg like dark lines of infantry on the march. It was nearing 10:00 P.M., the time the park closes for the night.

Those who study the unexplainable have noticed that there are several periods when the supernatural seems...well...more natural than others. Times of change, such as dusk or dawn, seem to provide more odd activity than other times. The change in seasons—summer or winter solstice, spring equinox, and, of course, when fall turns to winter and the dead try to change places with the living at the end of October—Halloween. Many believe that just before or after a thunderstorm is also a time ripe for the bizarre to occur, when there can be that elusive crossover from one world to the next, from the inanimate to the animate....

They wanted to visit the Armistead marker one more time before they left. He looked for it in the distance, and finally saw it outlined, a lone monument in the dark, with no one around it. They crossed the road and approached the monument. Though there was no one near it just a few seconds before, "...when I got near it, about five feet away, I was startled to see three figures at the stone."

His wife stopped their two boys and they all remained about six or seven feet away, respecting the privacy of the other visitors to the monument.

He described them as being uniformed in full Confederate garb, tin cups hanging from belts, blanket rolls slung over their shoulders, and each carrying a rifle-musket. Looking around, the writer pondered their virtually instantaneous appearance and wondered where they had come from since there were no cars on Hancock Avenue behind them and no cars parked on the Emmitsburg Road in front of them.

One of the figures was stooped over the stone and was reading, in a distinctly southern drawl, the inscription: "Brigadier General Lewis A. Armistead fell here July three,

1863." The man and his family remembered how he used "three" instead of "third."

To try to break the ice, the letter writer said, "Yep, that's where he fell." He did not receive the reaction he had expected: "They acted as if they never heard me, in fact, they never acknowledged the presence of any of us, and we were almost close enough to touch them."

When the first of the three finished reading, the fellow next to him started to sob. The man who did the reading stood, put his arm around his shoulder and said, "He was our brigade commander." He took his arm down, pointed into the dark void across the vast field before them and said, "We came from all the way down there and then back again." The soldier's sobbing continued.

Brigadier General Lewis Armistead monument.

Without ever acknowledging any other presences around them, two of the soldiers began to walk off to the right of the monument and one to the left, all headed toward the stone wall and the Confederate lines.

Being but five feet away it took only a second or two for the letter writer and his family to reach the marker. By the time they did, the men were lost to sight. Their equipment, which was jingling as they walked off, suddenly stopped making noise. It was as if they had walked through a heavy curtain that parted for them then closed again on the tragedy in which they'd faithfully played their parts—both in this time and in the past.

A couple was visiting in October 1994. They were regulars to the historic town, especially that year, and are reenactors. Both hold respectable jobs, he as a processing engineer and she as a library director who writes and also lectures on Victorian women's studies. They have had a few psychic experiences on Civil War Battlefields, in particular the Antietam/South Mountain area. She mentioned she believed reenactors and those associated with historic or battlefield sites are more open to psychic experiences, "because of our love and respect for the past." At about 8:00 P.M. that night, out on the road to Emmitsburg, they would literally come face-to-face with proof of that belief.

No doubt they were aware, as they drove southward on the road that bisects the bloody field across which Pickett's Charge advanced, of the scenes played out on either side of them during the battle and, in fact, in the actual road where they drove. They had to be aware of the random destruction dealt out by Union cannon firing down from Little Round Top on Pickett's men as they approached the Emmitsburg Road—"plunging fire" makes such a mess of flesh and bone. Or of the volleys of infantry fire laid down upon the heads of Confederates just as they tried to climb across the stout post and rail fences along either side of the road— men tumbling into the road to writhe in their death throes. And, being reenactors, they were acutely aware of the horror of those last few minutes, while what was left of

Pickett's men advanced up the slope toward the stone wall, heads bowed as if walking into a storm, and took volleys of infantry and artillery fire like deadly, hot hail.

As soon as they left the lights of town, they began feeling anxious and uncomfortable. As they reached the Codori Farm, they both talked about turning around. The husband remarked that, for some reason, although it was a clear, starry night, he found it was getting hard to see.

They had just passed the Peach Orchard and the car rolled on between the dark, undulating fields, across which Kershaw's South Carolinians marched toward Mr. Rose's Farm. Many would never come back, finding both death and sepulture around the farm. Beyond all reason, the woman sensed another presence in the car. Turning apprehensively, she was shocked to see an officer out of time, but perhaps not out of place, traveling along that dark, deserted road to Emmitsburg in the back seat of their car.[2]

Remarkably, or perhaps because of her experience as a reenactor, she had the presence of mind to notice details about the entity in the back. The figure she described appeared in his thirties with dark hair, a droopy moustache, and three days' growth of beard. She said he wore a blue, short "shell" jacket, half unbuttoned and a dark shirt. His shoulder straps were of a First Lieutenant. He sat there stock-still, like a clothing store mannequin. Then, slowly, almost ominously, his head began to turn. It stopped and he gazed directly into her eyes with a soulless expression.

Suddenly her husband wanted to turn around. He quickly made a u-turn in the road and headed back toward the lights of Gettysburg. It was then that he confided to his wife why he wanted to turn back: in his rear view mirror, he had seen a figure in their back seat.

She excitedly exclaimed that she had seen him too, and her husband made her describe exactly what she had seen. Her description matched his, except that he insisted the soldier wore high, cavalry-type boots. How in the world could he know that, she asked, since the soldier was seated in their car?

Because, her husband said, when they had stopped to turn around he saw him from behind walking back over the ridge by the road toward the Peach Orchard.

It appears that soldiers are not the only spirits trapped in time, forced by Whomever controls such things to toil endlessly and anon, walking roads they've walked before and inhabiting, seemingly forever, places where they've suffered. Civilians too, are caught in the cruel circular labyrinth that brings them back again to the places most traumatic in their lives.

Emmitsburg Road.

Again a young couple was driving south along the Emmitsburg Road, out from the comfort of the populated streets of Gettysburg and into the midst of the fields that drank up the blood of thousands of young men and boys of the Southland.

In his letter, the writer assured me that he has been extremely reluctant to believe in the paranormal and very skeptical about beings or forces of the supernatural. His fiancée, however, is a little more superstitious, yet neither had seen or heard or felt anything out of the ordinary. That was soon to change one Sunday evening in July 1998 in Gettysburg.

It was between 6:30 and 7:30 P.M. They had just left the outskirts of Gettysburg and had reached one of the places where the National Park Service has cleared the crops for the passage of those tourists wishing to cross the vast field where so much of Longstreet's noble corps was annihilated. There, coming from where the crops had been cut short was a group of about ten or twelve young men and boys, in column of twos. If one were to see such an organized group—at least in this world—one would look for the brown uniforms of the boy scouts; if one were looking for something from the Other World, one would expect to see the gray or butternut of the Confederate soldier, a vision of a phantom battalion, seen often before on the Gettysburg Battlefield.

But something about their clothing was odd. The writer described them as having Civil War period civilian or perhaps even "Amish" dress. One of the young men appeared to be the leader and was ahead of the column. He wore dark trousers, a tan colored shirt, and a dark vest which he wore open. On his head he had a brown hat with an upturned brim and satin hatband. Perhaps the oddest part (or at least odd from the point of view of what we would expect to see) was that they were not carrying military arms, but picks and shovels, as if they were some work detail. They also had packs on their backs and marched wearily as if returning from the fields of toil.

As the month of July 1863, progressed, the work of burying the dead became more odious each day. There was the heat and the rain, which only led to the more rapid decomposition of the bodies. The bodies at first were blackened from the sun and bloated from the gasses

building up inside of them; then, after they had deflated—
some in violent, horrid explosions when they were touched
for burial—the very flesh began to slough off as the boys in
the burial parties tried to drag them to their graves, the
stench nearly unbearable. Months later, after the military
burial parties had left, local men were recruited to dig up
the bodies from the North and re-bury them in the new
National Cemetery, and so the horrors for the overworked
burial parties started all over again....

The column was only about twenty yards from the road,
and so the writer got a good look at them. But his fiancée
saw them as well. They joked about how strange they
seemed, and kidded each other that they may have just seen
an apparition. Suddenly, as if realizing exactly where they
were, they got serious and decided to turn around just after
they passed the Codori House to see if they could find out
where the men were going. In ninety seconds they were
back at the site where the party had been seen...but the
oddly dressed boys and their picks and shovels were gone.

They looked at the Union side of the Emmitsburg Road,
toward which the column was headed...but there was
nothing but open fields. As well, when they searched the
Confederate side they found no trace of the dozen or so
boys dressed as if they had just finished up a day of hard,
undesirable labor.

Trying at first to explain their presence, the couple
ruled out reenactors since it wasn't the anniversary of the
battle and it was a Sunday night when most weekend
reenactors have gone home. Hard-pressed to explain the
appearance of what he called "farm hands" marching as if
in a work detail, the man certainly couldn't explain their
disappearance, except with a begrudging nod to forces
beyond comprehension: "I have never been a believer in
what I once thought was silly stuff," he wrote, "but after
what I saw and the feelings I have gotten here, I do believe
now that this place is very restless. Since this event took

place, we have often wondered what purpose would a group of civilian looking young men be in a reenactment?"

His last question has been answered by the historical fact of the preponderance of burial details in the month after the great bloodletting here, and by the modern fact that reenactors, after their great battles where "dead" men can rise when they are over, do not need burial details.

And finally from the fields that, for one long summer in 1863, where, after the battle men sowed the bodies of other men and to this very day reap their spirits, comes a tale of what some may call a "possession."

In May 1997 a Union reenactor was chaperoning his son's fifth grade class as they visited Gettysburg. To add to the color of their visit, the reenactor, in spite of the warm weather, donned his wool Union army uniform. One of the highlights for his son's class was the crossing of the fields, where Pickett's men advanced, with a Licensed Battlefield Guide. The guide, to dramatize the advance, lined the children up in two ranks, like soldiers. The reenactor/chaperon would march behind the line, acting as the "file closer." He was excited at the chance to walk Pickett's Charge since he had never done it before. And, for some reason, although he was at the back of the group and everyone's attention was on the guide, he had that strange sensation he was being watched.

He shrugged it off, and soon the little makeshift battalion of children were walking in the footsteps of the courageous young men who fought for the South.

When people walk the field of Pickett's Charge for the first time they realize that it is not flat, but full of swales and undulations that pull you below ground-level so that you cannot see the rest of the field. In spite of the warmth of the day and his wool uniform, each time he descended into one of the swales, he felt a noticeable drop in temperature. And while this was mildly unnerving, what bothered him most was the incessant feeling that someone was watching his every move.

They crossed the Emmitsburg Road and leapt the stone wall as Armistead's men had 135 years earlier. Once in "friendly" territory, the feeling that he was being watched left the Union reenactor. Questioning the rest of his party, he realized that no one else had felt that they were being watched, or the cold in the bottom of the swales. And on the way home he felt a haunting melancholy he had never experienced before upon leaving Gettysburg.

Little did he realize that, though he left Gettysburg, a part of Gettysburg never quite left him.

A few days after arriving home, strange things began to happen. Cupboard doors closed at night would mysteriously be open in the morning; clothing and jewelry would be moved and rearranged; magazines and books—especially ones about Gettysburg and the Civil War—would disappear and then turn up in odd places.

One night the reenactor and his girlfriend were downstairs in the family room. From above their heads came footsteps. Assuming one of the children had awakened, she went up to check. All were asleep in their rooms leaving them with no explanation—or rather, only one explanation—for the mysterious footfalls.

One evening they went out, making sure that all the lights in the house were off. They returned after dark to find the cellar light burning. He began to joke darkly that, after his crossing of the field of Pickett's Charge in his Yankee uniform, perhaps he had inadvertently brought back with him the discarnate spirit of a Confederate soldier who died trying to cross that very field he successfully had crossed under much more peaceful conditions.

The unexplainable happenings continued for a couple of months. He eventually began to call them, "Southern Revenge."

Finally, one day, he and his girlfriend were preparing to leave for a trip back to Gettysburg. As a joke they began talking about taking their uninvited "guest" back to

Gettysburg, where he belonged. His girlfriend called out to the spirit. They went to the car, opened the back door and invited him in. Upon their arrival in Gettysburg, they drove right to the Virginia Memorial, as he put it in his letter, "the starting point of our guest's journey to eternity." They told him he could get out of the car now, because he was home.

They finished their visit to Gettysburg and headed back home. As the writer put it, "I must say that it was nice to return home to a house that was just as we left it and we have not had a single incident since that day."

They still come to Gettysburg and he continues to wear the Union blue uniform as he explores the battlefield: to Devil's Den, to the Round Tops, Culp's Hill and Cemetery Hill. He goes to all the areas on the battlefield, "without any hesitation…except for that long open field between Seminary and Cemetery Ridges." Still he questions whether it is possible that "…some departed soul took offense to me walking across this hallowed ground in my suit of blue where he in his suit of gray had made his 'Grand and Final Assault'?"

They must grow as weary now, as they did in life, of the incessant marching, the constant fear, the never-ending stress of being timelessly and forever at war. So, it is not such a far stretch to imagine—for they were once just like us—them accepting a ride in such an odd-looking, horseless conveyance. For, as they say, apparently even in phantom armies, "It beats walking."

Walking Shadows

Our technology tells us that fluorescent lamps do not continuously provide light, but are actually flickering on and off at a rate that is just too fast for us to discern...reality at large is really a frequency domain, and our brain is a kind of lens that converts these frequencies into the objective world of appearances...there may be all kinds of things out there in the frequency domain that we are not seeing, things our brains have learned to edit out regularly of our visual reality.

–Michael Talbot,
The Holographic Universe[1]

For a while there was utter bedlam, in the Biblical sense of the word, in the formerly pastoral fields and farmlands, the once gentle valleys and rocky hillsides, and in the little town of Gettysburg itself. It could have been a model for Armageddon, the mythical battle at the End of the Ages. With unutterable savagery, men tore at each other for three long days inflicting the most horrific wounds upon one another, scattering flesh and bone and blood, ripping the very souls of their enemies from their mortal bodies, until, like primordial creatures, those who remained limped off to find solace and sustenance around their fires, to rest, to try and ponder their horrible deeds, their unnumberable sins, and their dubious redemption....

One hundred and twenty-nine years later, they would gather again....

The motion picture "Gettysburg" was filmed on and around the battlefields of Gettysburg during the summer of 1992. For several months during that summer and fall, the fields and farmlands, valleys and hillsides again felt the tramp of thousands of leather-soled brogans and witnessed the maneuvering of regiments of men and boys with a view towards their counterfeit mutual destruction. At night they would retire to their campsites, cook their coffee and meager meals, talk of home and loved ones, curl up in their little dog-tents, and await the morrows' mayhem just as their predecessors had.

Sometimes, during the filming, some of the units got a little "too into it," mysteriously seemed to take on the persona of the original units they portrayed, and "became" the soldiers and officers they recreated. With their heads filled with the knowledge most reenactors possess of their unit and their members, and seeing—from the inside—a reenacted battle, peering from under the short leather visor of a kepi or the broad brim of a slouch hat, it is easy to understand how one could get carried away.

There is, of course, always the possibility of that rare, but documented phenomenon known as a "walk-in," or "spirit possession," wherein a discarnate or earthbound spirit enters the body of a live human being. In degrees— usually never wholly—the spirit manifests itself in numerous ways. Sometimes a person suffers physical symptoms once associated with the possessing spirit; sometimes there are psychological symptoms; often, the possessing spirit is manifested merely in life-style changes: the host is suddenly drawn to art or music that never before interested him or her, or is drawn to an activity that seems as "natural" as if the host had been of that particular inclination forever....

Shortly after the filming I received a letter from Eric Johnson of California containing some thirteen pages of notes detailing numerous experiences he and friends had, as well as strange experiences he had heard others having.[2]

But since then I have received other letters containing additional experiences of individuals who were associated with the filming as extras. Interestingly enough, although it is obvious he is familiar with my interest in the ghost stories of Gettysburg, one writer from New York never mentions *Ghosts of Gettysburg III*, which contains the stories of the filming. Instead, he appears to be one of the percipients of two, and possibly three of the paranormal experiences mentioned in Johnson's notes. This testimony provides first person, primary source, eyewitness accounts to stories, which previously could have been dismissed as merely hearsay.

Around dusk on September 23, 1992, after all the filming for the day had finished, the young New Yorker was relaxing around the campfire with a few fellow reenactors. They were rocked from their evening reverie by the sudden discharge of two cannons near the movie set. They ventured over to where the cannons were "in park" as the Civil War era soldiers called it, and found that all the guns were cool and covered.

They returned to camp pondering the mysterious but unmistakable sounds of artillery firing. After awhile they turned in. Because of the cold, the writer of the letter slept in his car. At about 3:20 A.M. on September 24, he was awakened by the clanking of metal upon metal. He looked out the window of his car and was surprised to see a lone Confederate officer, which he identified by the gold embroidered sleeve markings. "He appeared to be waiting for a signal of some kind," and was looking in the direction of Gettysburg. The reenactor opened his car door to question what appeared to be another reenactor awake very early. When the light from the car's interior flashed against the mounted officer...he vanished.[3]

The young man questioned other nearby reenactors and two reported hearing something behind their tents, one at about 3:17 A.M. and the other at about 3:19.

On September 24, he and a fellow reenactor were visiting the famed Triangular Field. It was about 6:45 P.M., just about the time when dusk begins to shadow the former fields of conflict that time of year. For disputable amusement he shouted, "Get ready, boys! Here they come again!" He aimed a "pretend" rifled-musket across the fence and into the field.

His joviality was cut short suddenly by the sound of a muffled volley of musketry over the hill behind him. He and his friend rushed over to see where the anachronistic—

or rather impossible—sound had come from, and they were greeted with another muffled volley. Neither source could be found.

And yet, there was one place they didn't investigate for the source of the sounds. That's because it isn't a place they could investigate—at least not yet. It is the place where all the answers are. And the journey there is one-way. And the fee is high and non-refundable.

At about 7:15 P.M., as they were making their way through Devil's Den, they heard what sounded like a makeshift chorus of men's voices singing. Again, investigation revealed no source. At about the same time, they were startled by something sliding on loose rock. They looked up to see what they thought was another reenactor making his way down from the boulders that make up the Den. They called out to him, but received no response. They decided to climb up and assist him down the slippery hillside. As they were climbing up to him, they kept anxious eyes upon him, hoping he wouldn't slip again. As they watched him making his way carefully down…he disappeared before their eyes. As if a sudden disappearance weren't enough to convince them of what realm they had now entered, they continued to search for him for another 25 minutes.

The young reenactor returned to his car to sleep for the night. But in the comfort of his own car and on the usually silent campground situated on part of the battlefield, he was awaked by a distinct voice. Though a disembodied voice in his locked car may seem unnerving enough, the message it bore was even more ominous:

"Stay out of Devil's Den!"

Early that morning, he delivered some flowers and an orange ribbon to the monument to the 124th New York Volunteers—the "Orange Blossoms," from Orange County, New York. After his private ceremony honoring the brave men he portrays as a reenactor, he stepped back to take a photo. As he began to leave, he heard muffled voices coming from behind the monument. He approached the monument to greet the other visitors, but found no one.

These muffled sounds of conversation are heard often in historic places.

They are sometimes audio-taped when there is complete silence as sort of a "white noise" in the background of Electronic Voice Phenomena—recorded voices of the dead. And so, perhaps it was merely the remnant spirits of the soldiers who fought so courageously and bled so dearly on the very ground where their monument now stands, expressing their appreciation to a modern-day member of their resurrected unit, as Joshua L. Chamberlain wrote, with "Honor answering honor."

A second letter I received was from a man who works as an educational consultant for a large software firm. In October 2000, he had taken one of the *Ghosts of Gettysburg Candlelight Walking Tours*® and was reminded of some experiences he had during the filming of "Gettysburg." He said he was motivated to write in order to validate his experiences; did what happen to him happen to others as well?

It was that summer of 1992. He was reenacting the part of a lieutenant in a Midwestern Federal artillery battery. The first morning at Gettysburg his unit transported the guns to the battle site on the National Park where filming was to take place. Rangers greeted them and inspected the guns. Oddly, the rangers told them that their presence would "stir up the ghosts." I say "oddly" because the "official" Park Service position on ghosts is that they do not exist—at least, not on Gettysburg National Military Park. The writer continued: "We listened somewhat amused but not convinced as they recounted tales of ghostly sightings. By the time the week was over, I was convinced."

He continued by listing several stories I'd heard rumored but not substantiated: the mystical "rebel yell" emanating from woods where no reenactors were, echoing down time from where no humans existed—at least on this plane; muzzle flashes, again where no living soldiers were; and sightings of soldiers marching straight through other soldiers as if they didn't exist.

On the day they were filming the gory climax to Pickett's Charge, he was serving as a Confederate Infantryman. The directors told the units involved to advance just so far, then to halt so that they could set up the next shot. The regiment to the immediate left of the writer's regiment, for some reason, was choosing not to obey the instructions and continued to advance farther than told.

(I personally spoke to a member of the unit who said they just couldn't help themselves; it was as if some force took over and they had to continue the advance. Apparently, this happened several times.)

Finally the director dismissed the unit completely from the site. They began the shoot over again, this time without the misbehaving regiment. As the writer then put it: "On another take of this shot, the director called a premature 'cut!' and came storming down the Confederate line. He pointed at our unit and said, 'You fellas are OK, you did what I asked, it's that unit to your left that won't follow instructions.'"

The only problem was, there was no other unit to the left since he had "dismissed" them. No one else saw the unit on the left. But certainly the director apparently did, through his camera lens. And certainly they had been there…129 years before….

The next day the writer became a "galvanized Yankee." Reenactors will often bring both Union and Confederate gear to reenactments, since the drills, maneuvers and weaponry were virtually the same whether Yankee or Rebel, and will fill in whichever side needs men (or women!). His artillery battery was set up defending the position they were told to assault the previous day: the Union line on Cemetery Ridge during Pickett's Charge.

The two guns of the battery they had brought to Gettysburg from Illinois were split: one gun was posted behind Cushing's Battery on the left, the other near the replicated Bryan Farm on the right. The writer was in command of the left section. To his left, the entire Union line was crouched down behind a reconstruction of the famous stone wall. The guns were loaded and they were waiting to begin firing for the smoke generators to fill the field with historically accurate smoke. At that moment, the writer spied a lone Union soldier "shuffling" along behind the line at the stone wall towards the guns when he should have been lying prone behind the stone wall. If he was delivering a message, he certainly wasn't in a hurry. The writer expected one of the movie people to step in and get this guy to act the way he was supposed to.

He was wearing the uniform of a first sergeant in the Iron Brigade. As the writer related: "I also noticed how 'authentic' he appeared; particularly his gaunt figure and scraggly beard. This was an excellent impression, I thought." But he also wondered what a member of the Iron Brigade, which had fought itself out on the first day's fighting at Gettysburg, would be doing in Pickett's Charge, a recreation of the third day. The man was an historical anachronism.

"Now he was upon us and I went over towards him and was about to ask him: 'Can I help you?' However, before any words could be spoken he turned his dark eyes upon me and I was held speechless! He only looked at me for a couple of seconds while continuing his journey right in front of my loaded guns. I was too stunned to speak, but expected one of my artillerists to shout him away from the front of our muzzles. No one said anything!"

He watched as the sergeant continued down the line and passed within inches of the captain commanding near the Bryan barn. The captain never flinched or acted as if he'd even seen him. The soldier then turned left and disappeared behind the barn. The director shouted "Action!" and the guns began firing.

For three minutes, as had been planned, the guns fired, then ceased firing. The writer promptly chewed out his cannoneers for allowing the man to cross in front of loaded weapons. He was met with confused gazes. No one had seen any soldier crossing before the guns. The writer headed for the captain. The soldier was nowhere to be seen; that section and their captain had seen no one. The writer remained in the area long after the action had ceased, but never again saw the strange, dark-eyed sergeant from a brigade once fought to extinction.

If that was all that happened to him and his friends, that would be enough. But he returned the following weekend with two friends and camped in the campsite he had used before. Straw was still scattered about. They were the only beings there...or so they thought. One friend slept in the van they came in; the other in his own tent; the writer in his historically accurate "A" tent.

Sometime during the night, the writer heard what he described as two sticks of wood tapping together, then rustling in the straw near his tent and more tapping. The tapping and rustling alternated for several minutes, and the writer assumed it was someone who arrived late at night putting up their tent. But the noise went on too long.

He peered outside his tent to see who was taking so long in putting up a simple shelter tent and was shocked to see...no one. He realized also, as he looked outside, all noises ceased. Looking around he saw, quite far away, a lone reenactor sitting by a fire. He had the presence of mind to notice that the man was downwind and thus, was unlikely to be the source of windborne tapping and rustling. What happen next assured him the man wasn't.

He stood in front of his tent for several minutes waiting for the noise to return so that he could pinpoint it; all was silent. He returned to his tent and crawled inside.

He was just dozing off when the tapping and rustling began again, this time coming from within his tent, right next to him. He threw back his sleeping bag and realized—thankfully—that no one was next to him. But the tapping and rustling had moved to just outside his tent again.

Realizing from his watch that dawn was rapidly approaching, he decided to wait out the tapping until it was light enough to see. But as dawn broke, the tapping ceased.

He asked his two friends if they'd heard anything in the night: One said no, the other said, yes, he'd heard someone tapping wood, but fell back asleep.

Meeting up that morning with his friend who was a first sergeant in the unit that reenacts as the Iron Brigade he told him of his experience. The sergeant, like many skeptics, told his friend again that he thought ghosts were nonsense—then proceeded to relate a ghost story of his own!

It seems that he and his wife during their stay the week before were at the famous Copse of Trees after dark. His wife heard something—she said "someone"—moving around in the dark. The sergeant himself, as she was taking his photo, admitted he actually felt someone lean an unseen hand upon his shoulder. When they had the film developed, all the photos came out except for the eight they had taken at the Copse of Trees—those were black, except for the outline of what appeared to be his gold-rimmed glasses.

He mentioned to his friend how he had visited the Iron Brigade monument and since the letters were hard to read, had placed his hand upon the monument. Immediately a "cold shiver" ran through his body. The sergeant's reply bordered on the incredulous: Yes, he said, the same thing had happened to him the week before when he had visited the monument—and something strange happened to his wife as she visited the National Cemetery dressed in her Civil War style hoop skirt. She was passing over the Wisconsin section and felt a cold shiver. She looked down and saw the name "Andrew Miller." She moved on. In her wanderings about the cemetery, she suddenly felt another cold shiver. She realized that she had inadvertently moved back into the Wisconsin plot. She looked down. There was Andrew Miller's grave again.

His rank was first sergeant in the Iron Brigade, the same as her husband's rank and unit, and the very rank and unit of the writer's apparition of the week before.

After they returned home, his skeptical friend did some research on First Sergeant Andrew Miller of the famed Iron Brigade. What he found led the writer of the letter to a fascinating conclusion about the odd coincidences they were subject to during their visits to Gettysburg.

He discovered that after the Battle of Antietam, September 17, 1862, Sergeant Miller had made a horrible mistake. He had written to the wife of his unit's commander informing her of the death of her husband in battle. The commander's hometown had held an elaborate memorial service for him with his grieving wife heartbroken and distraught over the loss of her noble husband.

But Sergeant Miller was mistaken. His commander had only been wounded and survived the carnage on September 17, what has come to be known as the bloodiest single day in American History.[4] As the author of the letter put it, "We are to understand that our Sergeant carried the sorrow for his mistake to his grave...I can't help but thinking that all of these events are somehow tied together."

Death is a weighty burden to bear, whether it is our own or someone else's. And so one wonders, why is it men, by going to war, rush impetuously into its grisly embrace when Death, with absolute certainty, will come when it wants, to them....

God's Scythe

...Scientific study and reflection had taught us that the known universe of three dimensions embraces the merest fraction of the whole cosmos of substance and energy.

–H. P. Lovecraft

American Culture was vast and deep even a century-and-a-half ago, and more so because of the distance between shores. The diversity in cultures between North and South, as a matter of fact, was the root cause of the great fiery cauldron called the American Civil War.

And one thing that many historians often fail to include in their discussion of the American culture at the time of the Civil War was how religious a society it was.

There were several major revivals of Christianity in the 1840s, 50s and 60s, and the tendrils of this religious background intertwined with the more sordid aspects of armies and war.

Young men, whose mothers and fathers took them to church each Sunday and read the Holy Bible by lamplight in the evenings and said grace before each meal, suddenly found themselves in the company of other young men who were gamblers and drinkers and liars, who cussed and blasphemed and took the name of the Lord in vain. They heard about adultery committed, and stealing, and men bearing false witness against their neighbors, and coveting just about everything. The evils they had been warned about in the traveling camp meetings and in Sunday school they saw acted out in the army. At nearly every stop on the march or in every camp, out came "The Devil's Pasteboards,"—playing cards— and men gambled away tobacco and coffee and every greenback they owned. They heard women called all sorts of vile names, and men—especially officers—called names as well; they heard almost unbelievable stories of strange and wicked happenings; and when they visited some of the larger cities like Washington, saw that it was all true!

They also found themselves in the awkward position, as devout Christians, of having to level a rifle-musket at a fellow human being, one also created in God's image, and to pull the trigger and kill him. "Thou Shalt Not Kill," was drilled into virtually every young man, North and South, from his formative years, and while Sigmund Freud did not discover the curse of the subconscious mind until well after the Civil War, it was, no doubt, in existence.

Yet another tenet of the mid-19th Century Christian Revival was the idea of "full-body resurrection."

Many Christians believed that, at the "end of the age," Christ will come to earth again to judge the quick and the dead, who shall rise from their graves and be resurrected. An important part of this orthodox belief is that the body have all its parts so that the individual may enter the Kingdom of God whole.

When one is in battle, with shot and shell and minie balls flying every which way, it is very difficult to guarantee that one will escape unscathed and intact.

Heard on more than one occasion, when a man was unceremoniously separated from one of his limbs by a cruel shell or shot, was that he wanted the limb brought along: "Here," said one being carried off the field on a litter. "Bring me my leg and put it next to me. It has been an old friend and I do not wish to part with it now."

Native Americans had a related belief: in whatever form a human left this earth, that would be the form in which he would be doomed to wander Eternity. This is why, after a battle, the Native American women would roam the battlefield, slicing with knives the dead enemies' thighs so they could not walk through the afterlife; or decapitating them so they could not function headless; or chopping off feet and hands so they could never march to attack their people again, even after death. This explains the ritual mutilations of

George Armstrong Custer (a Gettysburg veteran himself) and his men after the Battle of the Little Big Horn.

So it must have been particularly horrible for some young man, schooled in the catechism of "full body resurrection," to awaken after the surgeon's knife had removed a damaged limb and to find that it had been carelessly tossed out a window, mixed with others' mangled, bloody, amputated limbs, carted away and buried or burned.

And so it must have been with one James McCleary of the Union artillery. Sometime before the battles there on July 2 and 3, on the easternmost crest of Cemetery Hill, Union artillerists had emplaced cannons within "lunettes"—the crescent-shaped mounds still embracing the cannons there that now represent the original gun positions during the battle. No doubt James pitched in with the boys, wielding pick and shovel with the two good arms he was born with, straining flesh and blood, muscle and sinew accustomed to the hard work in the artillery. He, like all his comrades, knew the lunettes could be a life-saving barricade between them and rebel bullets.

But they might not protect the gunners against other artillery shells, especially "plunging fire" with a trajectory that dropped them from above. Not much could defend against that, as poor James McCleary was soon to discover.

Beginning at about 3:00 P.M. on July 2, there was a classic "artillery duel" between Latimer's Confederate Battery on Benner's Hill and Wainwright's Federal artillery on East Cemetery Hill. The fighting was particularly savage, even for an artillery fight. Men were cut in half, disemboweled, had their heads torn off, had legs amputated, pieces of skulls, necks, shoulders and hands gouged out. Horses were torn to pieces or panicked, kicked their handlers in heads, stomachs, and faces, and ran wild. Shells struck rows of men lying in what they thought was safety behind rock walls and ripped dozens apart. Shot struck wooden gun carriages, driving pieces of wood and iron into men attempting to load and fire the guns. On more than one occasion, a shot landed in an ammunition chest, exploding its contents and separating for eternity the body parts of the men around it.

Lunettes on East Cemetery Hill.

Sometime during the fight, James McCleary was wounded in the legs. But in a battle where immortal deeds were done by mortal men, McCleary bravely, tenaciously stuck to his post. From another battery came "plunging fire." The Confederate fire was accurate. Fatally accurate for James McCleary. As he continued to work the gun his right arm was viciously torn off by an enemy shell. The limb landed somewhere near one of the lunettes James strained so hard to build just hours before. During the cleanup after the fight, heaven knows what became of the arm. It was thrown in amongst hundreds of other body parts, no doubt, and buried in some unmarked, unsanctified hole, or perhaps burned in one of the hideous, smoky pyres that dotted the field for weeks after the battle. The dauntless artillerist was last seen being carried off the field murmuring weakly about his missing arm. He died shortly and was buried in the Evergreen Cemetery, the civilian cemetery just a hundred yards or so from where his life's blood flowed freely from a traumatic amputation by cannon shell. He lies there still…but without his arm.

But, if one believes the whispers among the tour guides of the *Ghosts of Gettysburg Candlelight Walking Tours*®, when the earth was shoveled over his cold form was not the last time he was seen.

The guides and customers have seen and heard a number of mysterious, unexplainable things on East Cemetery Hill, from columns of blue lights over the statues of Generals O. O. Howard and Winfield Scott Hancock, to the distant, phantom sounds of soldiers cheering from the woods below, to gunfire echoing off Culp's Hill in the distance. But perhaps the eeriest occurs only at certain times—after a thunderstorm or during full moon when shadows dance a mournful waltz among the lunettes.

Along the darkened and dismal skyline the guide and her customers see a lone figure moving, then bending low as if seeking something near the batteries, then moving on. Closer he comes to the confused group, closer still, in the dim light of the moon or the reflected light off the low cloud cover, until he turns and a frontal silhouette becomes clear. The observers look, and everything is fine until one notices: "Look. He's missing…my goodness…he has no right arm."

And so we must wonder: until he is reunited with the missing body part, is the courageous cannoneer James McCleary doomed to wander East Cemetery Hill in his zombie-like trance, searching—forever searching—for the arm that will allow him Grace?

James McCleary Headstone.

The Shadow People

Far—as the East from Even—
Dim—as the border star—
Courtiers quaint, in Kingdoms
Our departed are.

–Emily Dickinson

We all know what ghosts look like, right?

Or, at least we *think* we know.

Visually, by common definition, they are whitish, amorphous, misty things that float about. Some say they can appear as an orb, if their energy is concentrated, or, in certain circumstances, can take the shape of beings associated with life: an animal, like a horse or dog or cat, or, especially disturbing, as a human being, dressed in the clothes he or she wore the last time they were seen on this earth.

But there are other creatures that appear to be ghosts, yet have not the form they should.

They have been called "Shadow People," or "Dark Ghosts," and their role is harder to ascertain.

Your standard, misty-gray "ghost," often will manifest itself in playfulness or mischievousness. "Shadow People" seem more reticent to interact. To some who have seen them, "Dark Ghosts," seem ominous. Some have even expressed the fear that these are indeed the evil spirits whose pranks are not merely mischievous but can meddle with the affairs of the living to a great degree.

Which begs the question: Are the dead capable of wreaking harm upon the living? It is more than just a schoolboy query from a tale told outside a darkened cemetery. The ancients thought the dead malevolent.

According to Alan Baker in *The Gladiator: The Secret History of Rome's Warrior Slaves*, the gladiators' combat unto death replaced human sacrifices previously practiced for the purpose of "nourishing the dead with the blood of the living." The practice was apparently widespread in the ancient world:

"The Romans, who imported ideas of the afterlife from Greece and Etruria, feared and respected the powers of the dead, as did many ancient peoples. They believed that on occasions they could gain entry to the realm of the living and perform all manner of mischief, including dragging people back with them to the Other World. These fears were to a large degree put to rest by various public and private ceremonies aimed at limiting the powers of the dead, and confining their return to Earth to certain days."

One of these days, of course, became "All Hallow's Eve," or Halloween.

"Although the dead were feared and respected, in the religion of ancient Rome they were not seen as inherently dangerous and aggressive. Their hostility was only aroused if the duties to them were not performed in the proper way. A dead man was seen by the Romans as a shadow emptied of substance, a 'lack.' It was with the spilling of human blood, the very fluid of life itself, that the dead were given back a transitory reality, and thus propitiated.

"The gods of the underworld (Dis Inferi) were said to be responsible for outbreaks of plague, which were seen as manifestations of their displeasure."[1]

Perhaps this is where we get the phrase, "Have some respect for the dead."

Indeed, "Shadow People" have been seen on the Gettysburg Battlefield.

"Gloria," a friend of mine for two decades now, admitted that she has always been sensitive to the inhabitants of the Other World. Indeed, she's had dozens of experiences. But some of the most confusing to her were the dark shapes she has seen. She consented to an interview and revealed the following:

I asked her when she saw her first "Dark Ghost."

"Probably at my house. Inside my house. [There were] scuttling shapes, across the floor at my house. And at Little

Round Top. I've seen things flit through the air too, not a shape but a creature. Strange, dark, shadowy things flying, flitting through the air."

Her house is on a section of the battlefield used primarily by cavalry.

It must be remembered that there is the National Park and then there is "The Battlefield" which is far more vast. The "fields of battle" are so much more extensive than just the government-owned "Battlefield," that it is a myth to think the National Park is the only place in and around Gettysburg where men fought and died. The town of Gettysburg has six or seven times more historic houses than the National Park; Adams County has probably a hundred times more historic structures than are found within the government boundaries. The extent of the fighting, suffering and dying is more extensive than the human mind can comprehend, and it extended into every back yard, outbuilding, parlor and chimney-corner within at least a five-mile radius of the center square of the town. The National Park doesn't have the market cornered on the battlefield because, as Napoleon once said, "A battlefield is anywhere a man can place his foot."

For Gloria there was another encounter with "Dark Ghosts," this time about eight miles west of Gettysburg on the road to Cashtown, at Flohr's Church Cemetery, one burial ground which Confederate soldiers, marching on their way perhaps to their own doom, passed, no doubt thoughtfully.

Others were with Gloria that evening. They saw the dark shapes several times that night: "The first time, I saw a dark shadowy thing fly from the church to the cemetery across the street. Then from stone to stone, or above the stones there was a dark shadowy thing."

They, like ordinary ghosts (if anything in the paranormal can be called "ordinary") can be found everywhere: "I've seen them fly through the air at Spangler's Spring." She recalled that, at times the barely illuminated background of trees would be blocked out by an even darker shadow, moving slowly, methodically along the tree line.

On another night, again a cemetery was involved, one that certainly weighed upon the soldiers' minds as they literally fought through it on a little hill just north of the Adams County Alms House.

"Potter's Field," The Alms House Cemetery.

Though the Alms House is long gone, the cemetery is still there on the hill, and older locals like to call it "Potter's Field," after the field purchased with the money Judas received for betraying Christ, land set aside for the burial of strangers and the poor.

For a few horrifying hours in American History, that little knoll and the cemetery assumed the manifestation of a roiling, bubbling mound of death. The name of General Francis Barlow of New York, who was seriously wounded there, was forever linked with the height, but, if bravery and suffering were the criteria for naming a battle site, it could have just as easily been called "Wilkeson's Knoll."

When part of Barlow's Division was placed upon the small hill, it represented the extreme right flank of the Union line on July 1, 1863. It was a perilous position at best, but it was the only high ground in the area and had at least that advantage. So Barlow placed his men and artillery on the hill.

Young Lieutenant Bayard Wilkeson commanded the artillery battery upon the knoll. He seemed to be everywhere on his white horse, adjusting his battery line, making sure his men had ammunition, checking with superiors, but most of all, encouraging his men and making sure they were getting the maximum effect with their pieces.

His efficiency was noticed by his superiors. Unfortunately, it was noticed by the enemy, too. In a rare instance, Confederate gunners were ordered to take out the active officer on the white horse. This they did. Wilkeson was blown off his horse horribly wounded. His leg was virtually amputated by a shell and hung by only sinew. It slowed him as he crawled to the Alms House for medical help, so he took out his pocketknife and finished the job. He later died of his wounds.

Barlow himself was shot in the chest and went down not far from the paupers' gravestones. His general's shoulder boards were spotted by Confederate Brigadier General John B. Gordon, and in the midst of flying lead and iron, Gordon dismounted and gave the apparently dying Barlow a drink from his canteen and ordered some of his men to move the stricken fellow officer into the shade. Gordon himself was no stranger to Death: Shot in the face at Antietam, he fell unconscious with his face in his hat and would have drowned in his own blood if some thoughtful Yankee hadn't earlier shot a hole in it to let the blood drain. Gordon arranged for Barlow's wife to pass through Confederate lines, he assumed, to claim her husband's body. Instead, she found her husband barely alive and nursed him back to health. Barlow was exchanged later in the war and fought in other battles and, after thinking his Confederate savior dead after reading his name on the list of those killed in action, ran into him again some decades after the war. Each thought the other had passed and so for them it must have been very much like a ghost meeting another ghost.

And a careful examination of the hill shows that the position was a bad one to begin with. The Union soldiers were easily flanked by overwhelming numbers of Confederates coming from the northeast, and once the rebel infantry got close enough to the side of the hill, the Union gunners couldn't depress their muzzles far enough to hit them.

Gloria also had a "dark ghost" experience on Barlow's Knoll:

"[The one at Barlow's Knoll] was probably the darkest black I've seen of any of these dark things. [It was] running across the road in front of us at Barlow's Knoll heading back toward the Alms House cemetery."

The government road makes a loop around the summit of the knoll; the old cemetery lies within the loop.

After driving around the loop and coming parallel with the cemetery again "it ran through my headlights to the cemetery. Adam [her passenger] saw the same dark, shadowy thing but he saw it in a different way than I did. I saw something low to the ground and he saw a tall figure running. So we perceived it slightly differently."

Or perhaps they were two separate entities each saw.

Gloria continued to explain that it was only fifteen to twenty feet in front of the car and moved about 2½ to 3 feet above the ground.

"And Adam saw a tall figure at the same time. We both looked at each other at the same time and said, 'did you see that?'"

And, most recently, Gloria had a most bizarre experience with the "dark ghosts."

She was home in her house near South Cavalry Battlefield. Safe in bed, she had the lights on and was about to go to sleep.

There, just a few feet in the distance, was what she described as a "black orb." She said it was about the size of a golf ball, and moved diagonally across the room, and floated upward. While watching it she questioned herself: it certainly looked like an orb before her—she had seen them before and had taken and seen photos of dozens of white orbs. Perhaps, she thought, even though it was perfectly round, it was an insect. But then it did something insects never do: it disappeared into the ceiling.

*　　　*　　　*

Others have seen the weird, dark shapes as well.

One engaged couple was visiting Gettysburg in July 1998. Every night they were in town they would ride out to Devil's Den and try to take pictures of the disembodied spirits said to roam the area.

For a haven, no place can be more amenable to the dead than Devil's Den at Gettysburg. If a sudden, horrifying death is what it takes to make the spirit linger, surely, this place— where men died from the concussion of bursting shells bouncing off solid rock to slam them fatally in the head—is a prime candidate. If, as some people believe, the very earth must contain elements that can capture the energy cast off by the living as they die, then surely a place filled with granite and silicon and quartz rock in overabundance would do. Certainly, where men grappled back and forth, engaged not only in the struggle for their own precious lives, but for the life of their respective countries, where in the balance was the future of the very world, if that does not qualify for the lingering-place of souls wondering for eternity the outcome of their struggles, then we cannot name a place….

It was night again. Each time they had visited Devil's Den the past few nights, the man brought his expensive camera. The camera would not focus. According to the woman, "What's strange is his camera would work in other areas at night."

Interestingly enough, paranormal researchers find that in an allegedly haunted place, their camcorders' automatic focus continually goes in and out of focus. It is as if something keeps passing between the lens and the subject, but there is nothing in front of the camera. Nothing visible, that is….

His wasn't the only camera that wouldn't work. His fiancée wrote: "…I decided to try my camera. I aimed towards the area of Plum Run but when I tried to push the button down it wouldn't move. I then turned around to take a picture of the boulders and the camera would work. I turned around facing Plum Run and once again, the button would not budge. Thinking this was strange, I turned around and tried taking another picture of the boulders and my camera would work. I did this a couple of times and it was the same each time…."

They ran into another family returning to their parked car who asked them, apparently jokingly, if they were looking for ghosts, to which the husband-to-be replied, "Yeah, all the time."

The mother of the family told them that they had just seen a group of soldiers moving through the field on Little Round Top. As they drove off, the man looked towards the area she had pointed out and saw what he described as "A huge black figure gliding down the hill. It couldn't have been human because of the rate of speed it was going."

She tried taking another picture of Plum Run when a sudden feeling came over her, something she said she never experienced before. She felt not just fear, but absolute dread; she felt the need to leave the place where Texans and Georgians fought New Yorkers and Pennsylvanians, where countrymen tore at each other to the death, and from where, for a few hours on July 2, 1863, God must have turned His face.

Devil's Den—named for the very antithesis of Goodness and Light—where men were shot and tumbled, helpless but still alive and feeling, down thirty foot rock walls to the earth below, or into some wedge of a crevasse between two boulders, to suffer and die and lie until their bones were found months after the battle. On the night of July 2, 1863, the very place wailed with the screams of the wounded and the dying.

She said, although it was a balmy evening, she experienced a "bone-chilling cold...throughout my body." Her fiancé also felt it when he seized her arms to help her back to their vehicle. In reality, she admitted that she was pulling him to the truck. By the time they reached the vehicle, she was crying uncontrollably and her heart was pounding. Her reaction escalated and she started to hyperventilate.

Fearing the worst, her fiancé drove from the area rapidly, but her frightening symptoms continued. They reached the Wheatfield and suddenly her reaction stopped.

The next morning they had their film developed. Not one of the photos taken at the Devil's Den came out. The negatives show a bright light on each frame when the photos were exposed, which would seem impossible since they were exposed in the dark. In closing her letter the woman admitted, "I cannot explain what happened that night at Devil's Den. Maybe I was caught in the middle of a ghostly battle reenactment. I know one thing. I left Gettysburg with a very unexpected experience that I will never forget."

And yet there are more examples of "dark ghosts."

There is an area referred to by older Gettysburgians as "pinch-gut." It is where Confederate Avenue crosses the Emmitsburg Road. Careful examination of the site will reveal to the observant visitor daffodils, whose roots remain for decades, indicating where some fastidious housewife attempted to brighten her yard, evidence of domestic settlement from centuries ago.

Nestled in the northern fork of "pinch-gut" is the Snyder Farm. One can easily imagine Mrs. Snyder, up at dawn, sweeping the doorstep when her attention is drawn by a strange, dusty, undulating mass approaching from the south. Slowly it materializes from the morning fog. In the fore she might discern mounted officers parting the mist. Behind them, a bright flash of color: the white and red and blue of the Federal Army's First Corps' battle flags. Perhaps she sees in the lead, surrounded by his staff, the doomed Major General John F. Reynolds spending his last few hours upon this earth. Of course, the same could be said for a large number of the men who trudged past her modest wooden farm house that morning, including men of the famed Iron Brigade, a unit composed of tough Midwesterners, distinctive in appearance because of their broad-brimmed black hats.

The unit won its nickname during the fighting in the passes of the South Mountains, just a few score miles to the south, during the Antietam Campaign. As they butted their way doggedly through the pass, oblivious to their own casualties, one of their commanders remarked, "My God, that brigade must be made of iron!" Military men latch on quickly to flattering comments about their fighting prowess and the First Brigade of the First Division of the First Army Corps became simply, "The Iron Brigade," and sealed their distinctiveness by ignoring the wearing of the little "kepi" headgear and brandishing the black Hardee hat, with its protective broad brim.

On July 11, 1995 a woman and her son were approaching Gettysburg from the south along the Emmitsburg Road. Despite the fact that the hour was late, they pulled to the side of the road to observe a strange cloud of mist in the darkened fields that once held the bodies of young men sacrificed—as they would say back then—on the altar of their country.

As they sat pondering the weird mist, they saw something even more bizarre. Emerging from between a distinctive bush and adjacent tree was, what they described as "A dark shadow." The woman continued: "We were quite surprised when this shadow started moving toward us."

The Emmitsburg Road and West Confederate Avenue.

As they realized that the "shadow" was approaching them, they also realized that the area where they stopped is a very lonely place, especially at night. And although in their haste to leave they could give only brief glances at the dark figure, she was sure of one thing: "The only outstanding feature was the outline of a wide brim hat."

By the time they reached the outskirts of Gettysburg they had convinced themselves that it must have been merely a shadow. But when they got to their hotel, as they were exiting their car, they overheard another couple talking in the parking lot. They had seen exactly the same dark shadow with a broad-brimmed hat at exactly the same spot on the battlefield.

The next morning the woman and her son drove back to the spot and parked. Inexplicably, there was no sign of the tree and bush between which they had seen the shadowy figure appear.

Less than a year earlier, a man who was a reenactor—by all rights someone who could recognize the image and outline of another dressed in Civil War era garb—was visiting Gettysburg on the 131st Anniversary of the first day's fighting. He and four friends had found the famous (or infamous) Triangular Field, scene of so many weird and inexplicable intrusions from the Other World. It was 8:45 P.M. They were about to witness, into their reasonable, logical world, yet one more intrusion.

As they entered the field which, 132 years and 366 days before had seethed with the fire and fury of mortal combat, they saw a couple, about 75 yards into the dusky field below them. The evening was cool for July and the field an oasis of calm. Until a strange intruder appeared.

From the right side of the field, a figure, roughly identifiable as human in shape, emerged from the woods and stone wall. From there it moved up across the darkening field at a "very rapid pace."

The reenactor described its movement: "It was literally at a fast walking pace with no leg or arm movement—all dressed in black from head-to-foot and it seems to be floating across the ground. Also very noticeable was there was no sound of running through the grass—there was complete silence!"

The couple before them noticed the figure as well. They suddenly turned and rapidly climbed the slope toward the gate. As they passed the reenactor and his party they threw up their hands and said, "We heard enough about this place. We're out of here!"

The dark figure "floated" diagonally across the weirdly shaped field. It drifted rapidly to a clump of trees with two flat rocks nearby and disappeared over a slight drop-off beyond.

One of his friends screwed up his courage and, in spite of the bizarre, dark figure's mysterious and even menacing appearance, volunteered to walk down to the spot where the apparition disappeared.

After five minutes of observation, he returned, like an efficient scout, with his report, unsettling as it might be.

He said when he reached the far side of the hill there were two "soldier-dressed" figures sitting on the two flat rocks near the clump of trees. Neither one spoke to the other; nor did they even seem to acknowledge the other's presence. Instead they just sat, seemingly rigidly fixated, staring down into the field which once drank in the blood of the noblest souls of both sections of our country.

After their friend's description, they all agreed that it was definitely time for them to leave. They vowed, however, to return the next day.

And when they did they discovered something that shouldn't have been. They attempted to reenact the supernatural action of the black figure. None could run just like the figure. None could copy the action of the dark apparition they'd seen the night before.

And finally, there was a woman who, upon visiting Gettysburg in 1994, felt compelled to walk the fields across which the men of Pickett's Division and parts of two other divisions marched in the futile charge that ended all Confederate hopes at Gettysburg.

She left from the Virginia Monument. It was 3:00 P.M., virtually the same hour when Pickett's men stepped off to eternal glory and eternal oblivion, when the woman began her trek into what she would soon discover was a walk like no other she had ever taken.

She was accompanied by her daughter who maintained a position about twenty yards ahead and to her right. She was impressed at first with the serenity of the beautiful autumn afternoon and a walk through a field alone with her daughter. That would suddenly change.

About halfway across the field, her daughter, who was still ahead of her, planted a small Confederate flag to honor the men slain in the very fields they now crossed 131 years later. As the woman walked past the flag for which so many men died, she felt something press against her right shoulder, "as if someone was walking shoulder to shoulder with me." She quickly looked to see if someone had joined her, but saw next to her only the open fields where Death once cut deep and wide into the heart of America. In addition to that, she "had a strong feeling or sensation to my left side and witnessed a shadow there and also a shadow right behind my left shoulder. They too were very close to me as if they wanted to keep in a tight formation."

As the men of Pickett's Charge began their advance, their orders were to "guide center." The commanders knew that when men began to get hit by artillery and fall they would leave gaps in the battleline. With the dust and smoke thrown up by exploding shells, tactics demanded they practically keep in physical contact: shoulder-to-shoulder. When men went down, there was a constant pressing together of shoulders. The loss of that pressure was ominous: it meant a dear comrade was wounded or killed. Thus, when men died, the space they left was closed quickly, at least on the battlefield. The vacuum left in the hearts of loved ones who remained behind in the South would never be filled. And, all along that mile long line, for the entire time they marched could be heard the orders of the sergeants: "Guide center! Close up! Guide center!"

She continued her description: "Their outlines were real. I saw the outline of the guns over their shoulders, the Kepi on their heads with their heads turned down and I felt that they were very sad. I'll never forget that feeling of sadness they conveyed to me."

Descriptions of the men in a Civil War assault often talk about the men bending their heads as they advanced, almost as if they were walking into a heavy rainstorm, as if the thin wool of their fatigue jacket and leather of the brim of their kepis would protect them from flying lead and iron.

"One by one they left me. I have a feeling that as these shadows left my left side it became the point of where they were killed in the battle."

As the distinctive shadows on her left fell away, the pressure on her right continued to the point of annoyance. Suddenly she said out loud, "Back off!" And, as if respecting her wishes, the pressure eased on her right shoulder.

But something more bizarre was about to happen: "A man appeared at my side. He was my height, a younger man with dark brown hair and dark brown eyes. He had long sideburns and had not shaven for at least a day or two. His hat was a broad rimmed hat, very worn and dark from dirt. He had black suspenders on over his undergarment of a shirt. It wasn't a true shirt, but more of a long sleeved Long John type undergarment. He carried his long gun over his right shoulder, and I remember his hand holding the gun. For some funny reason I don't remember anything below his waist."

And then there was a sort of communication between them: "Mr. Nesbitt, the thing that got to me the most out of all this is that this soldier, almost twenty yards from General Armistead's plaque, turned to me, looked right at me, and smiled. A very warm smile, as if he was telling me 'Today's the day!' He then stopped smiling, became serious in face, turned his head to look forward and then disappeared. In my heart I know that this is where he too must have died."

The experience brought her to tears as she sat down on the stone fence once used by the Union soldiers to defend against Pickett's Charge. Yet she described the ordeal as not scary. She ended it with a "warm, pleasant feeling."

She concluded her correspondence with some reassurance that, "These things do not happen to me, I don't believe in ghosts, but I could not deny nor would I ever deny what I had just gone through. I could not betray those sad shadows…."

*Starting Point of Pickett's Charge at the Point of Woods
and the Virginia Monument.*

The Ghost House

Well what is this that I can't see?
Ice cold hands taking hold of me.
I am Death none can excel;
I open the door to Heaven or Hell....

–O Death, Traditional

Many of the people who enter the *Ghosts of Gettysburg Candlelight Walking Tours®* Headquarters to purchase tickets for the tour inquire whether they will be allowed to enter a haunted house.

The answer to that question is simple...and ominous: "You're already standing in one."

All who take the tours pass, usually without knowing it, through the doors of our own haunted house. Customers are allowed to wander through areas where visions of spirit orbs and spectral children dwell; where long dead residents or perhaps soldiers, true to their duty unto death (and beyond) still practice their defunct lives and manifest themselves by talking, touching and interacting with employees and visitors alike. Other areas in the house, off limits to visitors for very good reasons, have revealed childlike, ghostly, spirit orbs playing games and taunting one another, and unseen hands playing tricks on employees. True, documented events have happened and continue to happen within the walls that once contained the bodies and souls of Confederate soldiers and Gettysburg townsfolk alike.

Even before reports of paranormal happenings began to emerge about the Tour Headquarters, employees began calling it "The Ghost House." After the last six years inhabiting it, all who work there have realized that the name "The Ghost House" is entirely appropriate...and all too prophetic.[1]

In 1997 *The Ghosts of Gettysburg Candlelight Walking Tours®*—established in Gettysburg in 1994 as the very first ghost tour company—purchased a building on the corner of Baltimore and Breckenridge Streets from which to conduct tours. Like many of the historic structures in town, it was built in stages. In 1834 a small building used as a carriage trimmer's shop appears on the tax rolls. According to the Pennsylvania Historical Resource Survey prepared by historian Elwood W. Christ, Jacob Heck was assessed $175, probably for the "one story frame shop" on his property in 1834. By 1837 he was assessed 2.6 times that much for improvements on the property. This would correspond with the building of the two-story brick section that fronts Breckenridge Street. That documentation makes it one of the older structures in the borough of Gettysburg.

1834–1837 Section of the Ghosts of Gettysburg Candlelight Walking Tours® Headquarters.

On September 24, 1849, Andrew Woods, a carriage trimmer and dealer, and his wife Sarah purchased the property and continued to own it through the maelstrom outside their door known to history as the Battle of Gettysburg.

The next increase in tax assessment does not appear until 1888 and corresponds to the construction of the section that faces Baltimore Street.

So to visualize the structure as it appeared during the battle, one must stand on Breckenridge Street and erase in their mind the windowless eastern gabled section to the right.

According to Christ's report, in July of 1863, the house became part of the Confederate battlelines that stretched through the town. "The second story of the house afforded sharpshooters a vantage point from which to harass Federal troops in the vicinity of the Rupp Tannery and along the Emmitsburg Road towards the Dobbin House." So, picture rifled-muskets emerging from the windows on the balcony roaring with fire and smoke, then being withdrawn to be reloaded. In fact, to the right of the middle door, there is a chip in the brick, made by a minie ball from the Federal troops near the cemetery.

Christ also reported that the Henry Comfort house, immediately to the north and the James Pierce house, across Breckenridge Street on the corner, both became temporary field hospitals, which would indicate that Andrew Woods might have seen his share of wounded and dead in and around his house as well.

Picture then, as you stand looking at the balconied section, the two story structure with Confederate soldiers wandering in and out, sharpshooters at the second floor windows firing away at Yankees several hundred yards behind you, and wounded rebels making their way into the house or down into the cellar of the structure to rest until their turn on the operating table.

Some would eventually be transported, either by their own army to safety in the South, or by the Union soldiers as prisoners to the Camp Letterman Hospital. Others would never leave the house on the corner—at least as living beings. Some, it appears, left a remnant of themselves to remain within "The Ghost House" to this day.

But to help your imagination, we have an eyewitness account of what it looked like just two days after the battle.

Leonard Marsden Gardner wrote *Sunset Memories: A Retrospect of a Life lived during the last Seventy-Five Years of the Nineteenth Century 1831–1901.* In it he described Gettysburg as it appeared on Sunday, July 5, 1863:

"The wounded had been removed but the dead lay unburied and the ground was strewn with abandoned muskets, knapsacks, canteens and other accoutrements of war. The houses were marked with shot and shell on both sides of the street. Some with ugly gaps in the wall and others with a well defined hole where the cannon ball entered. A frame building particularly attracted my attention. It stood in a position facing the Union front and the weather boarding from top to within a few feet of the ground was literally honey-combed with the minie balls. No boards were torn or displaced but thousands of neat round holes marked the places where the balls entered."

Gardner continues his narrative, specifically describing the corner upon which "The Ghost House" stands:

"Passing on I came to the point where Breckenridge Street connects with Baltimore. There a barricade was thrown across the street. Through an opening at one end I led my horse and remounting I rode on down the street. A few persons only could be seen on the pavements. A scene of desolation and death was presented all the way. The unburied dead and the mangled remains of human bodies, mingled with debris of broken gun carriages, muskets, bayonets, and swords, which lay around in confusion on that lonely street in the quiet Sabbath morning, was one of those pictures of desolation which will never fade from my mind."[2]

On March 26, 1866, Woods sold the house and lot to a cobbler and his wife for $1,000 cash. David Kitzmiller and his wife Mary owned the house for 26 years. When they moved into the house, they brought with them at least one child, Charles B. Kitzmiller. At least two Kitzmiller children—Eva

Jane and William Henry—were born in the house. And at least one Kitzmiller offspring associated with the house died: William Henry died on February 1, 1899, at 24 years of age. There were perhaps more deaths in the house.

A mysterious entry in the Kitzmiller genealogical record in the list of the children of David and Mary Ann states, "Babes—number unspecified." As well, while not giving a specific date of death, first-born George Edward was baptized just 12 days after his birth (when the Kitzmillers usually waited a year or so before baptizing their offspring) indicating that his survival was in question. But there is no death date nor burial site specified for George Edward, nor names, dates of birth or death for the "Babes—number unspecified." They seem to just disappear from the records of the family and the house.

If a visitor to the *Ghosts of Gettysburg Candlelight Walking Tours*® Headquarters would like to walk in the footsteps of a near tragedy, they can walk behind the property into the alley behind the Carriage House and trace the near dragging to death, in 1880, of 15-year-old Charles Kitzmiller.

According to a local newspaper, *The York Springs Comet*, "...Charles Kitzmiller (son of David)...living on South Baltimore Street [in the *Ghosts of Gettysburg Candlelight Walking Tours*® Headquarters], Gettysburg, met with what might have proved a serious accident. He was herding a cow in the alley, having a strap attached to the chain. He thoughtlessly looped the strap around his waist when off started the cow and dragged the boy from above Comfort's shop [the house just north of the Headquarters] out to Buckinridge [sic, i.e. Breckenridge] Street and thence to Baltimore Street, passing Pierce's Corner [Southwest corner of Baltimore and Breckenridge]."[3]

Someone caught the cow and released the young man before he sustained anything more than just a few bruises.

In 1888, David and Mary Ann built the Baltimore Street-facing section and replaced the outbuilding on the alley with a larger structure—now the Carriage House—between 1907 and 1912.

David died in 1914, and upon Mary's death the house passed on to the surviving children who sold it out of the family.

As with any history, mysteries remain. As with nearly every historic house in Gettysburg, mysterious happenings and unexplainable events abide, perhaps as evidence of an unsettled past and an uneasy present.

As you enter the house, you might be surprised. It certainly doesn't look like a "Ghost House." But in that first room a number of dark, unexplainable, paranormal events have occurred.

A manager at the *Ghosts of Gettysburg Candlelight Walking Tours*® was alone in the house one night. She was between tours and the phone had finally stopped ringing for a moment. The place was quiet...until she heard something entirely out of place. Echoing softly from the dark stairwell across the room—and apparently across decades of time as well—came footsteps. She heard them lightly descend, one step at a time, and could actually follow the sounds, as the footfalls came slowly down the stairs and stopped at the bottom. She peered into the darkened hall, but saw no one. She bravely walked around the information desk and cautiously peeked around the corner to the foot of the stairs. No one—at least no one visible—was there.

Two hours later, the manager was talking to a person at the desk and was listening rather absentmindedly, letting her mind wander a bit, unknowingly putting her mind in a state where it is more receptive to the supernatural. Slowly, from the darkness at the bottom of the stairs, out of nothing, there materialized a small boy, age 6 or 7. "He had dirty blonde hair," she recalled, and described him wearing a light shirt with dark pants and suspenders. He stood there, looking into the front room, at the oddly out-of-place (at least to him) information desk and strangely dressed (again from his point in time) people. Then, as suddenly as he had entered this strange world, he left it, before her eyes could pick up any more detail of what was clearly an impossibility anywhere else but in "The Ghost House."

Stairwell where the apparition of a child has been seen.

Beginning in the spring of 2002, a visible, tangible, moving reminder of someone—or something—has frightened a number of employees as they freshened up in the employee's restroom, tucked beneath the stairs to the second floor. First it happened to Katie, a manager at the Ghost Tour Company.

She was taking advantage of a lull between customers to freshen up. Another employee remained at the ticket sales counter. As Katie stood next to the closed bathroom door washing her hands, the small brass door handle began making a small clicking and squeaking sound that accompanies its movement. She had dried her hands within a second and reached down and turned the handle herself, expecting to see her co-worker standing in front of the door playing with the doorknob.

Door to the employee's bathroom.

She opened the door. No one—at least no one visible in this world—was standing there. She walked the two or three steps into the main room to see her co-worker seated behind the desk. Katie didn't even have to ask whether she had been playing a trick: there had not been enough time for the co-worker to move from in front of the bathroom door all the way across the room and behind the desk.

In June 2002, it happened again.

This time another employee was in the restroom. No sooner had she entered when the handle began to rattle and squeak. As she stood next to it rinsing her hands and watching it, the knob began to slowly, methodically twist. She grabbed the handle and threw open the door to discover the perpetrator—and no one was there.

And it happened to yet a third employee: again the familiar squeak and rattle; as she looked to the small handle, it turned; exiting the room revealed...no one.

In October 1997, psychic Karyol Kirkpatrick toured the house and recorded her psychic impressions which, when compared to the documented history—and recent paranormal events—are remarkable.

One of Karyol's first impressions was that of a child whom she said had died upstairs. We would upon occasions, she said, hear marbles rolling across a wooden floor (even though it was now carpeted) and witness other evidence of a child trying to regain a childhood that was cut short by ever-ravenous Death.

There is that mysterious entry in the Kitzmiller genealogical record of "Babes—number unspecified." And their first-born George Edward baptized so soon after his birth as if he was not expected to live the usual year they waited before baptism. Could the child Corinne saw be the same Karyol felt had died here? Could it be some long-dead child playing with the doorknob?

Indeed, there was even more recent evidence of a child spirit's playfulness in the very room where you stand to get your tickets.

A manager was working behind the desk along with another employee. She felt a strange touch at her back; then a tug; then she felt the back of her sweater pulled several inches away from her back. She turned to look over her shoulder and wondered how, without moving, she could have hooked her sweater on something. But there was nothing upon which her sweater could have been stuck.

Just then she saw her co-worker, eyes wide with astonishment. She blurted out, "I just saw the back of your sweater pull out all by itself!"

Later that evening the manager was closing up for the night, alone, at about 10:00 P.M. Like all older houses, "The Ghost House" has its share of creaks and groans. Creaks and groans are one thing—but witnessing something supernatural is another thing entirely.

She was turning out the lights. The house, as the lights are slowly being extinguished, does have a certain "feeling" to it: as it grows dark, you get the inkling that you need to hurry, that someone—or something—can't wait for

you to leave so that they may get on with their existence—
if that's what one could call it —in peace.

Moving from behind the desk and into the next room,
she casually looked into the darkened stairwell. Her eye
was caught by what she described as a small, glowing
"cloud," —ectoplasm—ascending the stairs. It was almost
as if, at 10:00 P.M., some ancient voice, not heard on this
earth for a century, had called, *Time for all good children
to come up to bed.* And they obeyed, like the good little
children they once were.

The upper floors of the *Ghosts of Gettysburg Candlelight
Walking Tours®* Headquarters are closed to our customers, but
the most active area up there is too dangerous to visit anyway.
The stairway to the attic is narrow and winding and the only
light is activated by a string at the top of the stairs. Even when
your eyes grow accustomed to the dark, lights dance eerily
from the openings under the antique tin shingles. The roof is
too low to stand upright anywhere in the attic, and, although
hot air rises into the attic, it seems that whenever you ascend
the stairs you are met by a cold draft on its way out. One could
easily become disoriented and imagine things up there. But
Rick Fisher, renowned ghost hunter and paranormal
investigator, doesn't need an imagination to see ghosts in "The
Ghost House." *He has caught them on videotape!*

Within the last two years, Rick has used his Sony Digital
Handicam to videotape strange phenomena in this house.

His technique is to set his Handicam on a tripod in the
oldest part of the attic, late at night when all activity—human
activity, that is—has ceased in the house, turn the camera on,
then leave. He returns when the battery is about to die, then
rewinds the tape to examine it for any anomalies.

Rick is a skeptic, and so is careful to analyze in detail
what he records. So far he has had three distinct recordings
of voices—known to researchers as Electronic Voice
Phenomenon, or "EVP"—in an attic where no one was.

One night, after placing his camcorder in the attic over the oldest section of the building, he returned to analyze it. Out of nowhere, recorded on the tape, came the frantic voice of a little girl trying to communicate what may have been the answers to all our fears about dying:

"*I'm alive!*" came her voice across the Great Chasm.

Then, shortly after that came a man's breathless voice calling, plaintively: "*Emily!*"

Listening more carefully, Rick then thought he heard the little girl's voice say her own name, "*Emily.*"

In another taping session, there was paranormal evidence that the house—and particularly the attic—was used during the battle. On Rick's videotape could be heard a distinctly frightened male voice imploring, "*Don't miss!*" Then comes a different man's voice immediately afterward commanding, "*Get me my gun!*"

And finally, Rick may have captured the only voices that accompany a video of spirits in the attic of "The Ghost House." *In this tape one can see, as well as hear, spirit entities communicate!*

It was Halloween night 2000. Rick's camera was set up in the attic, recording the last minutes of the tape. In the background can be seen the louvered window in the oldest part of the attic. Suddenly, from the lower right hand part of the screen come two white, glowing orbs—what some believe is spirit energy itself—one following the other, rising toward the upper left corner. Listen closely and you will hear a playful, childlike voice teasingly whispering, "*Catch me!*"

Could these be the spirits of the children Karyol Kirkpatrick sensed remaining in the house, the mysterious "Babes—number unspecified," of the genealogical records, still enjoying a game of tag stolen from them by Death?

Yet another incident occurred to verify the existence—or non-existence—of children no longer living on the second floor of "The Ghost House." Katie would keep her dog, "Chessie" on the second floor while she was working. Chessie loves her tennis ball and Katie was playing "fetch" with Chessie. She'd roll the ball along the floor and Chessie would retrieve it for more fun. Finally Chessie tired of the game. Katie rolled the ball to the other side of the room and Chessie just looked at it and lay down to rest. About thirty seconds later, both Katie and Chessie were surprised to see the ball, which had been stationary across the room, begin to roll towards the dog, finally ending up next to her. Someone in that room, after waiting to play for perhaps a century or more, apparently was not ready to cease playing with the dog.

And, like all children, they—whoever it is that remain in the house when everyone else is gone for the day—sometimes can get over-bearing.

Chessie is not a small dog, and like all dogs, is faithful and protective, confronting and barking at large men who she feels could do her family harm. Yet children can sometimes "not know when to quit."

On her lunch break, Katie went upstairs to spend some time with Chessie, since she had been too busy to visit her since she got to work. Katie got upstairs, looked all around for the dog and couldn't find her. She checked the door, and it was secure, so she couldn't have run out. Calling the dog's name, she finally saw that Chessie was hiding under the bed, a place she'd never gone before. It was as if, for the two or three hours Katie had left Chessie, the unseen "children" had hounded her, teasing, pulling her tail, playing, until the dog just had to get away. To this day the dog is visibly uncomfortable whenever she is on the second floor of "The Ghost House."

Walking through the small, arched doorway under the sign marked "To Tours" places you in the Civil War period section of the house. Erase in your mind the bookshelves, fan, and electric lights. Replace them all with gaslights or candles, perhaps some 19th Century furnishings, and antique carpets. But make sure that some of the carpets are bloodstained. Place Confederate soldiers in the corners and leaning up against the walls, exhausted, dirty, perhaps bloody, smelling like sulfur (from the black powder they used), sweat, and fear.

Karyol Kirkpatrick mentioned during her visit that she "saw injured persons and blood" and a couple of men hiding in the basement below your feet. She heard music and instruments. (It was common for fighting men of all eras to amuse themselves—when not fighting for their lives—with song and easily carried instruments like harmonicas.) She got the impression of men from Georgia and Virginia in the house. (Documentation proves that Georgians were the troops occupying this section of Gettysburg. Virginians may have straggled here from their lines on Long Lane just a few hundred yards to the west.) And she never mentioned Northern troops as being present.

She saw a woman in dark clothing who, she stated, "did not have it all together," but only as a ruse. She had a mission as a secret courier, acted crazy, and no one paid her any attention. She mentioned a woman named "Mary," who loved cooking—Karyol smelled mince pie—and she "received" the name "James," and heard a man talking incessantly about God.

Once through the first room of the Civil War section, you enter into the second (of three) rooms. Just to the right of the doorway was seen, what many people refer to as a "Shadow Person," or dark ghost.

An associate of the *Ghosts of Gettysburg Tours*® had just finished spending some time in that room. It was late at night and the building was closing for the evening. An unusually large number of customers had passed through that night since there had been a book signing. Researchers have discovered that, in order to increase your chances of photographing spirit entities, you must first fill a room with people, then empty it. It seems as if the entities return, after a large crowd has left, to see what was going on. Such is just what happened that night. The associate was behind the exit door pushing it closed and had turned toward the far wall. He was alone in the room…but not for long.

Out of the corner of his eye he saw the figure of a small woman, seemingly cloaked in a long, dark, flowing dress with a wide-brimmed, black hat, standing in the corner where the counter meets the wall. He stood for a brief moment, seeing her out of his side vision, afraid to look directly at her, since he realized that entities could sometimes only be seen through peripheral vision. Indeed, when he turned to confront the dark lady, she vanished.

Could it have been the mysterious "secret courier" who acted insane as a ruse that Karyol talked about? Or was it "Mary" the cook Karyol mentioned. Remember, in the long history of the house, there was a Mary whose last name was Kitzmiller, who lived in the house for years and years....

Katie also had a frightening experience with one of the Shadow People.

It was Halloween weekend, one of our busiest, when she came into the Carriage House after attempting to close up "The Ghost House." She was visibly shaken. She still held the day's paperwork in her hand, which was trembling. She said nothing for a second or two, trying to find the words, then blurted out, "There's a large dark…" Again she searched for the words. "Scary…man…or something in the book room."

My first thought was that we were going to have to call the police to arrest someone who refused to leave after closing. But something in Katie's face told me that this was no ordinary visitor.

"Did he leave?" I asked.

"I don't know," she replied. "The lights were all off and I was walking past the book shelves, and there was this huge, dark, form standing there that I had to walk around. Instead of going into the office, I came right over here."

Reluctantly, Katie accompanied me to check out the intruder. By the time we got there and turned on the lights, whatever it was had vanished. Katie pointed out exactly where it had stood in front of the bookshelves.

It is when things are busiest in their dwelling-places that the spirits are most active. Already dispossessed once out of their bodies, they react when they are again dispossessed of their homes...

The current kitchen area is the oldest section of the house, built as the original carriage trimmer's shop in 1834. It is closed to the public...and for good reason.

Karyol felt what she described as a great deal of strong, negative energy coming from one particular corner of the room nearest the door leading to the outside porch.

Rick Fisher, during one of his late-night investigations, had just set up his Handicam and aimed it at that corner of the room. Before he had an opportunity to turn the device on to record, he saw, through the small viewing screen, what he described as a huge, bright, basketball-sized spirit orb emerge from the door of the kitchen and rush directly at him and his camera before veering off. He said it was the largest orb he had ever seen.

Supernatural events did not begin with the purchase of the house on the corner of Baltimore and Breckenridge Streets in Gettysburg, Pennsylvania, by a company committed to the preservation and re-telling of stories of the paranormal. Ghosts may have been "living" in the house all along, throughout the fourteen decades since the Battle of Gettysburg. What we are sure of is the supernatural occurrences we can document from the recent past...and those yet to come in the house dedicated to the Ghosts of Gettysburg.

*Orbs in motion in the attic of The Ghosts of Gettysburg Tours®
Headquarters.*

Endnotes

Gettysburg Underground

1 See Nesbitt, Mark, *Ghosts of Gettysburg*, "The Tireless Surgeons of Old Dorm," pp. 53–57 for many of the ghost stories associated with Pennsylvania Hall on the Gettysburg College Campus.

Unquiet Rest

1 See Nesbitt, *Ghosts of Gettysburg V*, "Climbing to Golgotha," pp. 44–46 for a brief history of the fighting on Culp's Hill.

2 Ogden, Daniel, *Magic, Witchcraft, and Ghosts in the Greek and Roman Worlds* (New York: Oxford University Press, 2002.)

3 A similar noise has been heard by others in motel rooms around Gettysburg. One man claimed it sounded very much like the watch-chain his great-grandfather—a Civil War veteran—used to own. See Nesbitt, *Ghosts of Gettysburg II*, p. 77.

4 Moody, Raymond, M. D., *Reunions: Visionary Encounters with Departed Loved Ones* (New York: Villard Books, 1993.) Dr. Moody is one of the pioneers of life after death studies.

5 I was amused when a National Park Service spokeswoman stated unequivocally that upon the proposed site of the future National Park Service Visitor Center there had been no fighting or substantial historical actions. It was as if she wanted us to believe that the wounded crawling to the Baltimore Road from the battlelines stopped and made a mile detour around the acreage set aside for the new Center to be built 145 years in the future. That we should have such prescience.

6 Phelps, W. Chris, *The Bombardment of Charleston, 1863–1865*. (Gretna, Louisiana: Pelican Publishing Co., 2002) pp.

10–11. Phelps points out that the siege of Vicksburg lasted 47 days, and Petersburg, nine months. What Charleston civilians endured would only be surpassed by the German siege of Leningrad—800 days—during World War II.

Time's Pawns

[1] Cook, Nick, *The Hunt for Zero Point: Inside the Classified World of Antigravity Technology.* New York: Broadway Books, 2001, NY.)

[2] See Nesbitt, *Ghosts of Gettysburg III*, p. 20.

[3] See Nesbitt, *Ghosts of Gettysburg*, pp. 11–14 for the story of the missing body of Wesley Culp, who, some speculate, is buried in the cellar of the Culp House on the battlefield.

The Substance of Shadows

[1] See Nesbitt, *Ghosts of Gettysburg*, pp. 46–48 for the story of how Miller won the Medal and the ghost story that it spawned.

[2] George Clark, as quoted in Glenn Tucker's *High Tide at Gettysburg*, (New York: The Bobbs-Merrill Co., Inc., 1958) p. 276.

[3] *The Batchelder Papers*, (Dayton, Ohio: Morningside House, Inc., 1994) Vol. II, p.774.

Translucent Reality

[1] "The Breastworks at Culp's Hill," by Capt. Jesse H. Jones, 60th New York Volunteers, *Battles and Leaders,* (Secaucus, NJ: Castle,) Vol. 3, p. 316.

[2] Pfanz, Harry W., *Gettysburg: Culp's Hill & Cemetery Hill.* (Chapel Hill: University of North Carolina Press, 1993.)

[3] Connell, Evan S., *Son of the Morning Star.* (San Francisco: North Point Press, 1984.)

When Heaven and Hell Changed Places

1 Rollins, Richard, ed. *Pickett's Charge!: Eyewitness Accounts.* (Redondo Beach, CA: Rank and File Publications, 1994.) This book is made up entirely of personal accounts of many who participated in the charge and is as close to being there as one can get.

2 See Nesbitt, *Ghosts of Gettysburg III*, p. 27–28 for another documented story of mysterious passengers from another era hitching a ride in a modern vehicle.

Walking Shadows

1 Michael Talbot's incredible work *The Holographic Universe* (New York: Harper Perennial, 1991) sheds as much light on paranormal studies as it does on the nature of reality itself. His exploration of the ideas of Karl Pribram and other noted scientists is a wellspring for new ideas about the other half of reality: death.

2 See Nesbitt, *Ghosts of Gettysburg III*, pp. 21–28.

3 This event corresponds in approximate time and place when a security guard, as he questioned what he thought was a mounted reenactor portraying an officer, saw the figure and his horse dematerialized right before his eyes in Nesbitt, *Ghosts of Gettysburg III*, p. 21. As well, it appears to be the primary source for Johnson's notes and the story recorded in Nesbitt, *Ghosts of Gettysburg III*, p. 22.

4 Renowned photo-historian William Frassanito, discovered that the single day of fighting at Antietam yielded more casualties than any other in American History in his research for Antietam: *The Photographic Legacy of America's Bloodiest Day*, New York: Charles Scribner's Sons, 1978.)

The Shadow People

1 Baker, Alan, *The Gladiator: The Secret History of Rome's*

Warrior Slaves, (reprint: Cambridge, MA: Da Capo Press, 2002.)

The Ghost House

1 "Fate's Children," a story in Nesbitt, *Ghosts of Gettysburg IV*, recounts some of the history of the house, including the story of the phantom hand that opens and closes the back door, and details of Karyol Kirkpatrick's psychic investigation of the house. So many other events have happened since 1998 that an "update" on "The Ghost House" needed to be done.

2 Gardner, Leonard Marsden. *Sunset Memories: A Retrospect of Life lived during the last Seventy-Five Years of the Nineteenth Century 1831–1901*.

3 *The York Springs Comet*, York Springs, PA., June 2, 1880. All the information on the Kitzmiller Family comes from: *From the Danube to the Susquehanna: 350 Years of the Kitzmiller Family*. Some kind individual gave me the segment of the detailed Kitzmiller Family History. Unfortunately, the page with publishing information is missing. I will assume, however, that it can be found in the Adams County Historical Society's archives, as extensive and thorough as they are.

About the Author

Mark Nesbitt was a National Park Service Ranger/Historian for five years at Gettysburg before starting his own research and writing company. Since then he has published over fifteen books, including the national award-winning *Ghosts of Gettysburg* series. His stories have been seen on The History Channel, A&E, The Discovery Channel, The Travel Channel, Unsolved Mysteries, and numerous regional television shows and heard on Coast to Coast AM, and regional radio. In 1994, he created the commercially successful *Ghosts of Gettysburg Candlelight Walking Tours,* in 2006 and in 2011 the *Ghosts of Fredericksburg Tours.*

Made in the USA
Middletown, DE
25 June 2019